W9-CLZ-882

Green Plate Special

Sustainable and Delicious Recipes

Christine Burns Rudalevige

Islandport Press

Islandport Press
P.O. Box 10
247 Portland Street
Yarmouth, ME 04096

ISBN: 978-1-944762-14-8
Library of Congress Control Number: 2017933492

Publisher: Dean Lunt
Cover and Book Design: Teresa Lagrange/Islandport Press
Cover Photo by Gregory Rec
Back Cover Photo by Brianna Soukup

MaineToday Media Photographers: Jill Brady (24, 29, 69/bottom, 173), Yoon S. Byun (138/bottom, 158), Gordon Chibroski (VI, 16, 34, 63, 84, 108, 125, 128, 130, 151, 179, 180, 183, 187, 192), Derek Davis (I, III, IV, 5, 13, 15, 36, 95, 116), John Ewing (138/top), Whitney Hayward (13, 74, 82, 93, 149, 171), Ben McCanna (205), Shawn Patrick Ouellette (6, 23, 53, 58, 77, 87, 145, 155, 167), Joel Page (3, 33), John Patriquin (107, 135, 135, 164), Gregory Rec (103, 146), Brianna Soukup (60, 69/top, 113), Gabe Souza (26, 188), Carl D. Walsh (121, 127), Logan Werlinger (64)

Additional Photographer: Christine Burns Rudalevige (15)
Page 39, iStock: Svetlana Kolpakova

Printed in the USA by Versa Press

To my all-time favorite dinner companion, Andy.

Acknowledgements

I didn't know I had a book in me. This one was made possible by family and friends, farmers and fishermen, and editors and eaters I've known along the way.

I am indebted to the cooks who taught me to stir the pot with love, frugality, and ease: my parents, Alba and Richard Burns; and the women who guided them, Alma, Elizabeth and Mabel. I tip my toque to every chef with whom I've shared a tight commercial kitchen space. Each lent me their culinary knowledge and let me witness their technique. I especially thank Ross Morris of Trattoria Piatto; Scott Jones, Pattie Roche, Mollie Sanders Martin, Vanessa Seder, and Heather Milliman at Stonewall Kitchen Cooking School; and, Ali Waks-Adams, my partner in the Butter+Salt pop-up restaurant series.

This book amounts to nothing without local food producers. I strive to do the fruits of your labors justice on every green plate I serve.

To my food-forward friends—Elizabeth Sackett, Cathy Barrow, Lucile Duperron, Ann Light, Ellen Peters Otto, Patricia Brown, Mary Pols, and Carmen Greenlee—who kindly critique my work on page and plate, I will always raise a glass to you.

To my brothers, Shawn, Tony, Jim, and Ken, your backhanded compliments of my cooking are always welcome. And to my sisters, Kate, Laura, and Jolene, your daily encouragements are vital.

I extend many, many thanks to *Portland Press Herald, Maine Sunday Telegram "Source"* food editor, Peggy Grodinsky, who makes my Green Plate Special column better weekly. My deep gratitude goes to Maine-Today Media CEO Lisa DeSisto and the Islandport Press team who took a chance on this first-time author.

And to Andy, Owen, and Eliza, know that cooking for you is my honor and my joy.

Husk cherry and hot pepper upside-down cornbread, page 41

Green beginnings

Just what is a Green Plate Special, exactly? Well, it's like a Blue Plate Special, only greener in the sense that the food on the plate is better for the environment and your body.

A Blue Plate Special is a low-priced meal served by and loved in diners across America. What lands on the plate changes based on the time, ingredients, and inspiration the professional short-order cook staffing the grill has at her disposal. It's easy, affordable, and quick.

The *Green Plate Special* Cookbook whisks sustainable eating practices into familiar, tasty recipes so that home cooks can serve them up from their own kitchen counters.

My own move toward more sustainably-minded cooking started modestly with some Blue Plate Special-like experimentation in my kitchen. Fifteen years ago, with two small kids to feed and two demanding full-time jobs in our household, meal-planning was essential but often mucked up because of my frequent tendency to go off-menu. On Friday nights, I'd open the fridge at 5:30, assess what lay in the crisper and in the darkest corners of the pantry, and make do with what was on hand. There were victories—my kids still clamor for Switch It Up Asian Chicken Noodle Soup (106)—and there were utter failures that led to pizza delivery.

My young family spent extended periods of time living and traveling in England, France, and Italy. These trips opened my eyes to the values and flavors of locally sourced, fairly priced, humanely raised food. After I earned my culinary degree and steeped myself in my local food system as a farmers market manager, chef, and cooking teacher, my cooking style got consistently greener and my meals got much tastier.

Over time, I learned that my preconceived notions about eating green were outdated. Eating more sustainably doesn't have to be as hard as you think it is. If I can do it, so can you.

But before we get too far, let me come clean here. I still eat Ranch Doritos and strawberry Twizzlers when I am stressed out. I couldn't grow a tomato if my kids' lives depended on it, and I gag every time I empty my compost bucket. I am routinely fascinated by clever plastic food packaging designs, and I always enjoy a big, fat, juicy beef burger. I'd never refuse a spoonful of a decadent dessert, and I've been told that I use olive oil like a Greek—only olives don't grow on as many trees here in Midcoast Maine as they do in Thessaloniki.

So why should you turn to me for advice on greening up your eating habits?

Because I know your limitations. Intimately, actually, because I have the same ones. We have fixed amounts of time, money, and energy to devote across all aspects of our hyper-busy lives, and therefore, don't have the bandwidth to go whole hog on a sustainable eating lifestyle. But there is a more navigable path to green eating embraced in an à la carte menu of greener plates, served over time, and ultimately making rich contributions to a more sustainable food system for our children's children.

For many of us, green eating raises a few questions: Can I afford it? Do I have the time to pull it off? Do my habits really make an impact? How do the small changes made by 10, 25, or even 50 slightly sustainable cooks compare to the concerted efforts of a single vegetarian who grows her own food, prepares it without the help of fossil fuels, wastes nary a potato peel, and never forgets to put reusable bags into her bike's panniers before cycling to the market for incidentals?

Getting solid answers centers on a distillation of a wide range of data collected about farming practices, food policy, transportation costs, and food waste management. And this data needs to be translated into manageable, actionable tasks that everyday cooks can easily integrate into their daily routines. I've taken a stab at that translation in the short essays in this book, adapted from my "Green Plate Special" column in the *Portland Press Herald/Maine Sunday Telegram* "Source" section, which I've been writing since July 2014.

I've spent years exploring the underpinnings of more sustainable ways to think about, source, cook and not waste food. I have tried to break them down into digestible chunks so they can be consumed according to every cook's circumstances on the days they choose to use them.

I've identified the ones that reasonably dovetail into my own eating regimen, adopted the ones my family finds palatable, and put off others that don't fit—at least for now. At this point I can rest easy knowing that my own family eats greener and greener with every new habit I embrace. I've tapped my formal culinary training to create the 112 balanced recipes included in this book. Every recipe makes at least one green eating point come alive on the plate.

"Greener eating involves making tradeoffs involving the foods we love: where we buy them, how we serve them, and how often we enjoy them."

Greener eating involves making tradeoffs when it comes to the foods we love: where we buy them, how we serve them, and how often we enjoy them. We've all made these kinds of tradeoffs over the course of our lives, whether we recognized them as such or not.

Take my dad, for example. In the 1970s and '80s, when I was growing up in Lee, Massachusetts (a small town in the western, more rural part of the state), he consumed eight Oreos a day. He had four after he'd finished his carpenter's workday and four more before he went to bed. He dunked them into fresh milk from High Lawn Farm, taken from Jersey cows pastured a little over a mile from our house, and delivered to our door (sometimes all the way into the fridge) in returnable bottles by Georgie the Milkman.

The cookies' highly processed ingredients, their packaging, and the miles they traveled to land in our snack drawer weighed down their overall cost on the environment, for sure. But the milk—locally sourced from an operation employing sustainable farming practices, and presented in reusable containers—balanced the snack's green eating quotient. Not that my dad made that kind of calculation at the time.

I wouldn't dream of asking my father to give up his Oreos. But I can tell you that these days, I have a better understanding of the high cost of processed foods on the environment and our health. In the college town in midcoast Maine I now call home, there are homemade cookies under the glass dome on the counter more often than there are Oreos in the snack drawer. The milk in the fridge is almost always local and sometimes even comes in glass bottles.

We need to face up to the undeniable facts about the unsustainable manner in which many of us get the majority of our food. Grocery stores and processed foods are, in fact, convenient. Feedlots render cheaper meat. Plastic clamshell containers protect delicate foods as they travel long distances, and plastic water bottles help immensely with on-the-go hydration. Cooking is not the matter of life and death it used to be. Leftovers aren't always as welcome as they are the day after Thanksgiving. And wasting food is not only acceptable in modern American life, in most cases, it's just how it is.

Which brings me back to the point of this book. I will show that by simply tweaking established meal planning, shopping and cooking habits just a

Grilled lemon thyme buttermilk biscuits with strawberries and cream, page 25

bit, any cook can make these recipes, and the resulting plates of food will be more sustainable over time. For example, Lemon and Herb Spatchcock Chicken (104) helps turn out two other meals later in the week—Second-day Chicken, Mushroom and Collard Green Wraps (105) and Switch It Up Asian Chicken Noodle Soup (106). This menu Plan-over cuts down on fossil-fueled shopping trips, maximizes your productivity in the kitchen, and reduces food waste.

Likewise, if you can recognize the local farmers market beets with their greens attached in September, you've found a cheaper option to the grocery store variety grown further afield—and you've got two ingredients (the beet itself and the greens) instead of one to work with in recipes like the Roasted Beet Reuben (67) and One-Pan Salmon with Spicy Creamed Greens and Tomatoes (130). Sustainable eating can actually make your life easier.

I'm not perfect: I fall down in my local food pledge with bananas, lemons, and avocados. Like me, if you can pinpoint which foods you can't give up even though they have to travel long distances to get to your plate, you can pledge to use every last bit of those items in things like Banana Walnut Waffles (24) and Lavender Lemon Posset with Candied Lemon Peel (152).

Finally, if you reclaim products you previously considered to be food waste—the rinds of hard cheeses grated over pasta; the heels of yesterday's bread; or, carrot, celery root, and parsnip shavings as a by-product of a vegetable heavy beef stew—you can turn them into green plate specials like Parmigiano-Reggiano Broth with Ravioli (47), Veiled Country Lass (150), or Garbage Finishing Salt (186). Each of these recipes will cut back on what ends up either on your compost pile or, worse, in your local landfill.

I've been a good cook (and an excellent eater!) long enough to know that the conversion to any type of culinary practice has to be positively reinforced at the eating end of the equation. The first step in using this cookbook is figuring out what you want to eat. The recipes are here to pique your interest and whet your appetite. As you move through the list of ingredients and the recipe instructions, you'll pick up tips and techniques that will help you become a more sustainable cook.

So pull up a fork. Allow the pages that follow to talk and walk you through the process of eating a little bit greener as you go. It's a shorter journey than you fear, and it makes a bigger difference than you think.

Christine

30 ways to think, shop, cook, and eat just a bit greener

Lists are more satisfying than good chocolate. Well, maybe not, but close. Lists provide concise directives for moving toward a goal and a sense of accomplishment as you master a task and tick it off the list. This list comprises my top thirty steps to a greener kitchen.

1. Plan for leftovers you'll actually want to eat. (Read "Plan-overs," 8.)
2. Buy a market basket or bag that makes you smile so you don't forget to use it.
3. Shop for fresh food once a week. Thereafter, make due with a stocked pantry. (Read "The Green Pantry," 6.)
4. Avoid the packaging pitfall of single serving foods. Plain yogurt by the quart is cheaper, more adaptable, and involves less plastic than yogurt delivered in six-ounce cups.
5. Pick a simple DIY project that trims something processed and packaged from your life (Kathy's Multi-Grain Crackers, 137).
6. Learn what produce is at peak this week, buy twice what the recipe calls for, use half and freeze half. (Read "Use Your Freezer as a Green Eating Vending Machine," 55.)
7. Help create a market for ugly produce by buying it to use when baking or making soup (Roasted Farmers Market Seconds Soup, 49).
8. Buy local chickens whole. (Read "One Healthy Local Chicken Does the Trick," 102.)
9. Once a week, use meat as a flavor-boosting condiment to vegetable forward dishes rather than hunky main events (Shredded Beef, Sweet Potato, and Black Bean Empanadas, 91).
10. Find cheeses made within 50 miles of your home that match your favorite foreign counterpart. (Read "Local Cheese Is Greener Cheese," 134.)
11. Use whole grain flours to ramp up sweet and savory all-purpose flour recipes. (Read "Eat Whole Grains, Preferably Local, for Breakfast," 10.)
12. Switch from white sugar to local sweeteners. Every time you reach for the sugar bowl, ask yourself "Can I use honey or maple syrup?" (Read "Local Sugar Substitutes Sweeten Things Up," 154.)
13. Swap tea bags for loose tea leaves and a strainer. Stop using coffee pods.
14. Change from paper napkins and paper towels to reusable cloth ones. Put a little vinegar in the wash to keep them fresh.
15. Invest in a manual food mill and a mandolin. Either can change the texture of a vegetable you don't know into a dish you can recognize (Lobster and Corn Wontons with Shredded Vegetables and Spicy Corn Broth, 57).
16. Match your pan's circumference to your stove's coils and cover pots to cut energy use by as much at 40 percent.
17. Use preheating and cooling down ovens for melting butter, setting crumb crusts, warming bread and toasting nuts (Maple Pecan Cream Tart, 157; and Spiced Maple Custard Pie, 159).
18. Line pans and baking sheets with a reusable silicone mat instead of tin foil or throw away parchment.
19. Keep three quart, pint, and half-pint mason jars with clean lids on hand at all times for storage purposes.
20. Make a big pot of something plain—rice, barley, beans, lentils, tomato sauce—on a Sunday and use it three times, three different ways that week.
21. Master soups made from bits you find in the vegetable bin the day before you head to the

market. Make a double batch and freeze half in lunch size portions. (Read "Sustainable Stone Soup," 46.)

22. Attempt a quick pickle with whatever vegetable is in your crisper drawer right now (Bulgogi Burgers with Quick Pickles and Spicy Mayonnaise, 97).
23. Master a simple pie/tart dough recipe. Keep one in the freezer (Kale Rabe and Potato Tart, 52).
24. Never buy breadcrumbs. Blitz French bread heels, sliced bread ends, and extra burger buns in a food processor and store in the freezer (Orecchiette with Cauliflower, Pancetta, and Breadcrumbs, 100).
25. Designate a refrigerator shelf as the "Eat Me First" zone, so that all who enter the ice box looking for food can help reduce food waste.
26. Save your bacon fat to add flavor throughout your week (Bacon, Buttermilk, and Blue Cheese Dressing, 172).
27. Keep a running bag of bones in the freezer for future stock making. Also keep onion skins, celery tops, carrot peels, and parsley stems for the same use.
28. Don't dump any liquid that could be used to add flavor to another dish. Mushroom soaking liquid, the last two tablespoons of beef stock, tea gone cold in the pot. Freeze them in ice trays with abandon and label, label, label.
29. Understand that food packaging dates are arbitrary. (Read "Understanding What a Sell-by Date Really Means, 72.)
30. Forgive yourself if you aren't the perfect green eater today. Start again tomorrow.

The green pantry

"Mise en place" is a French culinary term that translates to "putting in place." In restaurant kitchens, each line cook prepares her "mise" for each shift. She makes sure she's got all the ingredients she needs to prepare the dishes on the menu, they are prepped for use according to the chef's instructions, and stored according to food safety standards.

In a home kitchen, especially in a green one, the same concept applies. For a home cook looking to get more out of the sustainably sourced foods purchased weekly and waste as little as possible, keeping a pantry, fridge and freezer full of well-preserved staples is key.

There is both a range of conditions and a variety of vessels in which any food can be stored in a green kitchen. This chart is a snapshot of where in my larder the food sits and how it is contained. Organizing your pantry in a similar fashion will ensure you have the staples on hand to use the recipes in this book.

A few things explained: farm eggs that have never been refrigerated can sit on the counter, but once an egg has been refrigerated, it should always be refrigerated. All pieces of cheese should be individually wrapped and placed in either the cheese drawer or in a covered container as cheese will soak up flavors of other refrigerated foods around it. Neither maple syrup or oils will freeze. Tomatoes should be stored on the counter if you are going to eat them fresh but can be preserved in the freezer for future use if they are cored and frozen individually before being placed into a container.

IN THE CUPBOARD

In a bowl or basket:
garlic
onions
potatoes
shallots
sweet potatoes

In a glass jar:
apple cider vinegar
baking powder
baking soda
cornmeal
dried beans
dried chili peppers
dried fruit
dried herbs
dried mushrooms
honey
lentils
neutral oils
oats
rice
spices
sugar
vanilla beans
white flour
white wine vinegar
whole grains

In a dark bottle/jar:
fish sauce
coffee
olive oil
loose tea
vanilla extract

In the original packaging:
anchovies
canned tomatoes
coconut milk
chickpeas
noodles
nut butters
pasta
sardines

In a reusable container:
chocolate

ON THE COUNTER

In a bowl or basket:
apples
bananas
kosher salt
black pepper

In a dark bottle/jar:
red wine

In the original packaging:
eggs (see note, page 6)

ON REFRIGERATOR SHELF

In a glass jar:
bacon fat
hot sauce
mustard
nut flours
nut oils
simple syrups
white wine
whole wheat flours

In a dark bottle/jar:
yeast

In the original packaging:
bacon
bread
butter
buttermilk
cheese
cream
eggs
milk
yogurt

IN THE CRISPER

In a bowl or basket:
ginger
leeks
lemons
limes

In a reusable container:
fresh herbs
hearty greens

IN THE FREEZER

In the original packaging:
ground beef
ground lamb
ground pork
maple syrup
peas
shrimp
whole chicken
wonton wrappers

In a reusable container:
berries
bread crumbs
herbs in oil
nuts
nut flours
pie dough
stock, chicken
stock, corn
stock, Parmesan
tomatoes
wheat germ

Plan-overs

I did not coin the phrase "Plan-over." I stumbled upon it after my friend Sarah, who was weeding out her mother's cookbook collection, gifted me a lovely little hardback from 1960 called *The I Hate to Cook Book* by Peg Bracken. It has recipes for things like "Something Else to Do with New Potatoes Besides Boiling Them and Rolling Them in Melted Butter and Parsley" and quirky illustrations of perfectly coiffed but scowling women pulling off culinary shortcuts to minimize their time behind the stove.

Sarah passed this book along to help me better understand that not everyone enjoys being in the kitchen as much as I do. On page 29, Bracken scornfully assesses how "home ec-sperts who made straight A's in advanced cream sauce" changed the reputation of loathly leftovers to be celebrated "Plan-overs." They're leftovers you actually want to eat because you planned ahead to do something new and interesting with them.

"Thanksgiving turkey is the pinnacle Plan-over."

Thanksgiving turkey is the pinnacle Plan-over. When the 20 people in my immediate family on the Burns side gather, the bird we buy is never meant to last just one meal. We plan accordingly typically roasting a 20-pounder and a couple of extra breasts so there is enough meat planned-over to make sandwiches to fuel our respective rides back down the Massachusetts Turnpike.

There is no good reason we can't take the same tactic with Thanksgiving sides. Take local fingerlings, which are particularly fetching at that time of year. Here's how it works: Buy ¾ of a pound for each person you have to feed. That allows for a ¼-pound portion for each person for three meals running.

All the potatoes get boiled together to start. One-third is tossed with a vinaigrette that mimics the flavors of your roasted turkey, another third is sliced and pan fried with green onions for Friday's breakfast, and the remaining third is flattened and oven fried in olive oil for dinner on Saturday (Plan-over Fingerling Potatoes, 51).

If your family sits in the mashed potatoes camp, plan on closer to one pound of local russet potatoes per person to allow for peeling. Boil and mash them as you normally would, but remove ⅔ from the pot before stirring in milk and butter.

Make a hearty soup for Friday's dinner by frying bacon and softening onion and mushrooms in its grease, and adding equal parts mashed potatoes, broth and a few seasonings of your choice. Mix the last of the Plan-over mashed potatoes with sautéed cabbage for a breakfast of Bacon Bubble and Squeak Cakes (92) on Sunday.

Green Plate Special Plan-overs are clearly marked throug-hout the book with a green plus symbol (+). The success of any Plan-over hinges on portion control, so if you've got big eaters at the table, you may need to adjust how much extra to make in order for there to be enough food to produce the second suggested recipe. My best advice on that front is: plan accordingly.

All cooking temperatures are in Farenheit. If using table salt instead of kosher salt, please halve the amount.

Breakfast & baked goods

Christine

Eat whole grains, preferably local, for breakfast

Did you know, statistically speaking, most people trying to make changes in their eating habits start a new regimen on a Monday morning? Consider today a Monday, the day you're going to start getting more local, whole grain products into your life in general, but first and foremost onto your breakfast plate.

Eating local bread made from local whole grains helps a body cut back on processed foods, the miles your food has had to travel to your plate, and the plastic packaging used to keep it fresh until it got there. So by all means, use a local whole wheat baguette to make avocado toast and try out a new local flour to make breakfast flatbreads (Bacon, Greens, and Egg-In-The-Hole Breakfast Pizzas, 17) but for the love of oatmeal, don't discount whole, cooked wheat berries as a breakfast food.

The final lap in my formal culinary training was an 18-month stint on the line at a regional Italian restaurant called Trattoria Piatto in Carlisle, Pennsylvania. The pasta was made from durum wheat flour, the one traditionally used by Italians. But my favorite wheat-based dish was a salad made with farro, an ancient grain still in its berry form that we boiled softly in large batches and tossed with a simple vinaigrette and seasonal vegetables. The farro released the tiniest bit of starch, allowing us to mold the salad using a section of PVC pipe to sit prettily on the plate. The magic of farro for me lies in its satisfying chew.

Farro was the gateway grain that opened my eyes to using whole grains for every meal, including breakfast.

I boil a big pot of whole wheat kernels on the weekend (barley, emmer, farro, kamut, rye, spelt, or wheat berries work well too) and use them throughout the week when a hearty breakfast is in order (Warm Whole Grain Breakfast Bowl with Pears, Cardamom, Almonds, and Cherries, 11), a salad requires substance (Harvest Mason Jar Salad with Grains and Greens, 73) or a simmered dish needs to stretch for an extra eater (Clams with Grains and Baby Kale, 123). This cook-once-use-many-times method of locally sourced grains increases the green quotient of my meals.

Maria Speck, author of *Ancient Grains for Modern Meals* and *Simply Ancient Grains*, outlines the grain-to-water ratios and cooking times for any grain you'll find at the market. She advises soaking the kernels first, simmering them in plain water in a heavy-bottomed pan with a tight-fitting lid second, and adding salt at the end of the process. Once the grains are soft but still chewy, it's best to drain off the water, slap a lid on the pot, and let it sit for 10 minutes as most whole wheat kernels bloom after a bit of steam.

Storing cooked whole grains is an even easier prospect. After bringing cooked grains to room temperature, store them in airtight containers in the refrigerator for five days or in the freezer for up to three months.

Warm whole grain breakfast bowl with pears, cardamom, almonds, and cherries

Whole grain berries of all varieties fill you up and keep you going. While the berries are typically used in savory dishes, the maple syrup and sautéed pears make these bowls a sweeter breakfast item that get balanced by the tart cherries.

Serves 4

+ Plan-over grains for Harvest Mason Jar Salad with Grains and Greens, 73 and Clams with Grains and Baby Kale, 123

2 cups raw farro, rye berries, or wheat berries

2 tablespoons unsalted butter

2 ripening pears, chopped into bite-sized pieces

⅓ cup maple syrup, more for drizzling

½ teaspoon ground cardamom

¼ cup chopped, toasted almonds

½ cup dried cherries

½ cup Greek yogurt

To cook the grains, which can be done well in advance, soak them for 8 hours in cold water. Drain off soaking water. Put grains into a large pot with 8 cups of cooking water. Bring the pot to a boil, reduce heat, and simmer until grains are soft but still a bit chewy (35 to 40 minutes). Drain cooking water. Put drained grains back into the pot, cover, and let them steam for 10 minutes.

In a 10-inch skillet over medium heat, melt butter. Add pears and cook until slightly softened (2 to 3 minutes). Add maple syrup and cardamom. Cook for 1 minute. Add 2 cups of cooked whole grains, almonds, and dried cherries. Cook, stirring, until grains are heated through. Serve in warm bowls and top with yogurt and a drizzle of maple syrup.

Scoop remaining grains into an airtight container and keep in the refrigerator for up to a week. They also freeze well.

How to test out a new-to-you flour

Test out a new flour—buckwheat, rye, or white whole wheat—in a pancake recipe. Little product or time is spent, but its chemistry vis a vis other ingredients, taste and texture are noticeable.

Better blankets for your pigs

Yes, I serve Pigs in a Blanket for breakfast. I also served them during the cocktail hour at our wedding. It was the only item the groom insisted on. I've made them occasionally since as well, always running with the classic combination of Hillshire Farms L'il Smokies and Pillsbury Crescent Rolls. Recently stopped in my tracks by the realization that targeted philanthropic campaigns by food manufacturers like Boxtops for Education are vehicles for pushing processed food on kids, I've developed this homemade riff on the old classic. And if you don't eat meat, this dough works well for crescent rolls, too.

Makes 24
+ 8 Plan-over crescent rolls

1 cup all-purpose flour (plus more for kneading)

1 cup whole wheat flour

2 teaspoons baking powder

1 teaspoon baking soda

1 teaspoon kosher salt

4 tablespoons cold unsalted butter, cut into small pieces

½ cup grated sharp cheddar cheese

⅔ cup buttermilk

2 teaspoons honey

6 all-natural hot dogs

Preheat oven to 400°. Line a baking sheet with a silicone mat.

Sift flours, baking powder, baking soda, and salt into a bowl. Rub butter pieces into dry ingredients until mixture is crumbly. Stir in cheese until evenly distributed. Make a well in the center of the dry ingredients. Add buttermilk and honey. Stir to combine and let sit for 5 minutes. Divide dough in half. Wrap one half tightly and refrigerate for up to 3 days. Let the second half of the dough rest.

Cut each hot dog in half lengthwise then cut each half into 3 equal pieces.

Turn dough out onto a well-floured surface. With floured hands, press the dough into a rectangle ⅛-inch thick. Cut the rectangle into 24 small triangles, each with a 1-inch base and 2-inch sides. Roll each triangle around 1 piece of hot dog. Place pigs in a blanket on lined baking sheet with 2 inches between them.

Bake until golden brown (10 to 14 minutes). Cool slightly before serving.

NOTE: If making crescent rolls, after pressing dough into a ⅛-inch thick rectangle, cut dough into 4 smaller rectangles. Cut each small rectangle diagonally into two triangles. Start at the wide end and roll each piece of dough into a crescent and bake for 14 to 16 minutes.

Christine

Why pay six bucks for a dozen eggs?

Local eggs from pastured chickens provide an easy path to greener grub.

Yes, they are pricier than the grocery store variety laid by caged birds, but you're getting fresher, better tasting eggs. Plus, you're buying into your local food system six bucks at a time and supporting heritage breeds with cool names like Plymouth Rocks, Australorps, and White-faced Black Spanish.

Pastured eggs differ from commercial ones because a significant portion of the hens' diet comes from a variety of grasses and the bugs inhabiting them. This outdoorsy cocktail colors the yolks a vibrant, almost neon, orange. Many pastured poultry farmers adhere to pesticide-free practices, supplement their hens' diet with non–genetically modified feed, and refrain from widespread use of antibiotics, but not all are certified organic.

A fresh egg has a high yolk and a tight white. The albumen, the egg white, in fresh eggs contains more carbon dioxide than in old eggs, which makes the white cloudy and firm.

There is debate about whether fresh whites are better for whipped-egg baked goods like meringue, soufflé, or angel food cake. A fresh white separates from its yolk more cleanly, which is a good thing as even a tiny bit of fatty yolk can prohibit the whites from frothing appropriately. But the proteins in older, more relaxed whites tend to hold onto the air beaten into them better. Perhaps with this particular egg debate, it's six of one and a half dozen of the other.

Fresh eggs are best for poaching, frying, and scrambling. Older eggs are better for hard or soft boiling as the inner membrane of the eggshell relaxes its grip on the whites as the eggs age, making them easier to peel.

All eggs are laid with what is called the cuticle, or "bloom," a natural coating on the shell that seals its pores and prevents bacteria from entering the egg. Commercial eggs are power washed, stripping the bloom. Local eggs generally have only the hay into which the egg was laid gently brushed off before being placed in the carton.

The United States is one of the few places in the world in which eggs are refrigerated, a practice that further makes the shells porous. Once you refrigerate even a pastured egg, you've got to continue to keep it cold. But if I know they've never been in the fridge, I keep them on the counter.

A bowl of multicolored local eggs sitting on my counter makes me smile. But baking with them makes me scratch my head.

Recipe-writing standards assume any egg is Grade A large, unless otherwise specified. Local eggs come in all shapes and sizes because a mixed-breed flock lays them with hens sitting at different points in their production cycles.

In that case, a kitchen scale or a measuring cup and a bit of mental math will help you achieve the recipe results you are looking for in airy breakfast creations. The USDA sets the weight of a Grade A large egg at just around 2 ounces, with the yolk comprising one-third (about .7 ounces) and the white taking up two-thirds (about 1.3 ounces). By volume, two large eggs generously fill a ⅓ cup measure; two whites are nearly ¼ cup; and each

How to tell a rotten egg?
If you fear a raw egg is off, drop it into a glass of water. If it floats, it's rotten.

yolk is just about a tablespoon. Note my "around," "generous," "about," and "nearly" qualifiers.

Your local eggs may or may not line up with the same weights and volumes as commercial ones. If a custard recipe calls for two large eggs, and the volume of two local ones is too little but three is too much, lightly beat three eggs in a measuring cup and pour off the amount in excess of ⅓ cup and save it for another use.

When working with local eggs, it's good to be fleggsible.

Bacon, greens, and egg-in-the-hole breakfast pizzas

The cut-outs in this bread pull double duty: First, the nesting hole keeps the eggs from running all over the pizzas. Next, because the whites hit the hot pan, they get fully cooked while the yolks stay runny. I bake the cutouts alongside the pizza and dip them into the yolks.

Makes 4 personal pizzas

4 slices raw bacon, chopped

¼ cup chopped yellow onion

4 cups chopped greens (spinach, kale, chard)

½ cup grated Italian cheese (mix of mozzarella, Parmesan and fontina is best)

½ recipe Any Occasion Flatbread dough (recipe next page)

Oil to prepare pans

4 eggs

Red chili pepper flakes

Preheat oven to 425°.

Place bacon in a large skillet over medium-high heat and cook until crisp on both sides. Remove bacon from pan to drain on a recycled paper bag.

Pour off all but 2 tablespoons of bacon grease from the pan. Return pan to medium heat, stir in onions. Cook until soft (2 to 3 minutes). Stir in greens and cook until wilted, (1 to 2 minutes). Remove from heat and stir in bacon and cheese.

Divide dough into 4 pieces, form each into a ball, and roll out each one to be a circle with a ⅛-inch thickness. Coat 2 baking sheets lightly with oil. Place two rounds of dough on each sheet. Use a 2-inch round biscuit or cookie cutter to cut out a hole in center of each piece of dough. Place cutouts elsewhere on baking sheet. Bake for 5 minutes.

Remove par-baked dough from oven. Crack an egg into each hole, spread ¼ of greens mixture around each flatbread. Sprinkle red chili pepper flakes over each pizza. Bake until egg whites are set (5 to 10 minutes). Serve hot.

Any occasion flatbread

If you want to use whole wheat flour, increase amount of yogurt slightly (how much will vary), as whole wheat flour absorbs more liquid.

Makes 4 flatbreads
+ Plan-over 4 flatbreads

3 cups flour (all-purpose and/or whole wheat), more for kneading

3 teaspoons baking powder

1½ teaspoons kosher salt

2 cups plain yogurt

Olive oil

Optional toppings (flaky sea salt, chili pepper flakes, za'atar, poppy seeds, sumac)

Whisk flour(s), baking powder, and salt in a medium bowl. Use a fork to stir in yogurt. The dough will be crumbly. Dump it and any flour remaining in the bowl onto the counter and knead for 6 to 8 minutes so that the yogurt completely hydrates the flour. If the dough is wet, sprinkle more flour into dough while kneading. Cut the dough into 8 equal portions. Form each piece into a small ball. Roll out each piece to ¼-inch thickness.

Use four rounds to make Bacon, Greens, and Egg-in-the-Hole Breakfast Pizzas (17).

To cook flatbreads, place a cast-iron pan over high heat and use a pastry brush to lightly coat with olive oil. Place one flatbread into the hot pan. Cook until the dough starts to form bubbles and is brown in spots on the bottom (2 to 3 minutes). Flip and cook 2 to 3 minutes on second side. If using toppings, brush the top of the flatbread with oil and sprinkle with your topping(s) of choice.

Cool breads completely. Store in an airtight container for up to two days. These also freeze well. Reheat in a 250° oven for 4 minutes if room temperature or 10 to 12 minutes if frozen.

Eggs poached in buttery tomatoes, onions, and cumin

In this recipe, Moroccan shakshuka meets celebrated Italian cook Marcella Hazan's brilliantly simple buttered tomato sauce. Farm eggs get gently poached in a cumin-scented sauce made from frozen (or canned if necessary) plum tomatoes. Serve with plain couscous or crusty bread.

Serves 2 to 4
+ Plan-over sauce for pasta

6 tablespoons unsalted butter

1 teaspoon cumin seeds

6 cups peeled plum or Roma tomatoes (about 12 frozen ones, skins removed)

1 large whole onion, sliced

Kosher salt

4 eggs

2 tablespoons finely chopped chives, green parts of scallions, or parsley (optional)

Red chili pepper flakes (optional)

Melt butter in a 10-inch skillet over medium heat. Add cumin seeds and cook until fragrant (1 to 2 minutes). Add tomatoes, onions, and ½ teaspoon of salt. Cook, uncovered, for 45 minutes. Stir occasionally, mashing any large pieces of tomato with a spoon. Adjust for salt as needed.

After 45 minutes, remove half of sauce to cool and store in an airtight container in refrigerator for future use.

Bring the remaining sauce back to a simmer. Crack an egg into a small bowl, and use the bowl to gently place the egg into the simmering sauce. Repeat until all four of the eggs are in the sauce. Cover and poach the eggs until the whites are firm but the yolks are still runny (5 to 7 minutes). Remove the pan from the heat. Optional: sprinkle chives or scallion greens and chili flakes over top. Serve immediately.

Egg, chard, and cheese poof muffins

The women in my family served Cheese Poof at every bridal and baby shower we threw when I was growing up. The original recipe was handed down to my cousin Jean by her mother in 1979 in a handwritten cookbook of family recipes. Jean had moved with her new husband to Phoenix, Arizona, and was making frequent calls home to ask "Now how do I cook . . . ?" I've greened up the recipe with local milk, eggs, and cheese and a healthy dose of leafy greens. We used to cook it in a big ceramic bowl, but baking it in muffin tins cuts down on oven time and therefore energy use.

Makes 12 muffins
+ Plan-over chard stems for tartines, 71

2 cups whole milk

4 eggs, separated

1 teaspoon prepared brown mustard

1 teaspoon kosher salt

½ teaspoon well-ground black pepper

6 cups ½-inch cubes of day-old hearty bread

1 cup small diced local cheddar cheese (about 6 ounces)

⅓ cup unsalted butter, melted

1 pound of kale or chard, leaves torn from stems and chopped

Whisk the milk, egg yolks (reserve the whites), mustard, salt, and pepper in a bowl big enough to hold all of the recipe ingredients and still fit into your refrigerator. Add the bread and cheese, stir to combine, cover, and set the bowl in the refrigerator for at least six hours or as long as overnight.

Preheat oven to 375°. Coat a 12-cup muffin pan with melted butter.

Beat the reserved egg whites to stiff peaks. Remove the bread mixture from the refrigerator. Stir in chopped greens and fold in beaten egg whites. Divide the mixture evenly among the muffin cups. Pour ½ teaspoon of melted butter over each muffin.

Bake until the top and sides are golden and the centers only slightly jiggly (about 20 minutes).

Remove from the oven and allow muffins to sit for 10 minutes before serving warm.

Spicy crab and arugula omelet

With this recipe I've pulled in many of the sustainable eating habits I tout in this book such as understanding that local eggs are best (14), using garbage salts to amp up flavors (182), eating smaller portions of meat (86), and understanding the impact of eating fish (110).

Serves 2

4 eggs

4 scallions, green parts only, thinly sliced

1 teaspoon Garbage Finishing Salt (186)

2 tablespoons butter

1 garlic clove, minced

Large pinch of dried chili pepper flakes

¼ pound Jonah crabmeat

1 cup arugula leaves

Whisk together eggs, half of sliced scallions, and ½ teaspoon Garbage Finishing Salt in a medium bowl.

Melt 1 tablespoon butter in medium non-stick skillet over low heat. Add garlic and chili flakes. Cook for 1 to 2 minutes, stirring constantly. Pour into a bowl and combine with crab.

Melt the remaining tablespoon of butter in the now empty skillet over medium heat. Pour the egg mixture into the pan and cook until the eggs are lightly set (2 to 3 minutes), lifting the omelet occasionally to let the uncooked egg run underneath and set. Add crab mixture, arugula, remaining sliced scallions, and remaining ½ teaspoon Garbage Finishing Salt to the center of omelet. Fold the sides of the omelet over the filling, cut omelet in half, and serve hot.

Christine

Buttermilk: shake it, make it, and bake with it, but don't waste it

I managed the Farmers on the Square Market in Carlisle, Pennsylvania, during its 2011 season. Even when we were pitching canopies in pouring rain, I still believed that job to be one of the most fun I've ever had, second only to being a soda jerk behind the fountain at McClelland's Drug Store in Lee, Massachusetts, when I was fourteen.

As an outreach mechanism for the market, I taught a class to young children and their parents called "No-Thank-You Bites" at the local library. On a picnic blanket I laid out ordinary farmers market fare (peaches, cucumbers, carrots) and extraordinary foods (lovage, kiwi berries, green zebra tomatoes). To gain entrance to the class, kids agreed to take one bite of any food before they could declare it distasteful.

To keep small hands busy during the 30-minute class, I passed around two mason jars of heavy cream to be shaken, one into whipped cream for berry dipping; the other into butter for slathering on local crackers and buttermilk for sipping. Heavy cream when agitated long enough yields a 1:1 ratio of butter to buttermilk.

Brilliant, one mom declared. This process would allow her to make a batch of biscuits (Lemon Thyme Buttermilk Biscuits, 25) without buying buttermilk and wasting what she didn't use. I knew exactly what she meant. I, too, had neglected nearly full quarts of buttermilk until they went off and then down the drain.

But I've since learned what my grandmothers already knew and forgot to tell me: buttermilk is a wonder liquid. It can elevate the flavor of chocolate cake and the rise of pancakes and waffles (Banana Walnut Waffles, 24); tenderize chicken in a marinade; and provide creaminess to salad dressings (Bacon, Buttermilk, and Blue Cheese Dressing, 172) or a certain something you can't quite put your finger on in mashed potatoes.

There are three types of buttermilk. The kind produced in my class, from straight cream, is called sweet cream buttermilk. If you add a yogurt culture to the cream before churning it, you get both cultured butter and cultured buttermilk, which is tangier than sweet cream buttermilk. Heating low-fat milk with active bacterial cultures to sour and thicken it makes the third type, also called "cultured," the kind most widely available in stores.

You can simulate buttermilk, in a pinch, by mixing a tablespoon of white vinegar or lemon juice with a cup of low-fat or whole milk. The chemistry works, but seasoned buttermilk users say you can still taste that sharp acidic edge of the lemon juice or vinegar in the biscuit or scone.

Real buttermilk is always a tastier bet, and taking steps to use it before you lose it makes it your greenest option. The recipes here can help with that. And if there remains some in the bottle after making them, freeze it in ice cube trays for premeasured quantities in the future.

Buttermilk tip
Shake one pint of cream in a quart jar. First you'll get whipped cream. Keep shaking and eventually ½ cup of butter will separate from ½ cup of buttermilk.

Multi-grain homemade pancake mix

This recipe comes from a dear family friend of my editor. Her parents keep jars of this mix at their summer home in Vermont, where there is always a large pancake-hungry crowd for breakfast. The "other" flour in the mix can be a combination of ground oats or ground millet or rye and/or buckwheat flour. Try toasting some whole millet lightly in a dry sauté pan before adding it to the mix for a bit of crunch.

Enough for 9 batches of pancakes

Pancake mix:

- 4 cups whole wheat flour
- 3 cups white flour
- 5 cups other flour (see recipe note)
- 8 teaspoons baking powder
- 4 teaspoons baking soda
- 2 teaspoons kosher salt

Pancakes:

- 1 cup buttermilk
- 1 tablespoon melted butter or oil
- 1 egg, lightly beaten
- 1 cup pancake mix

To make the pancake mix, whisk all the ingredients together and store in a jar in the refrigerator.

When you are ready to make pancakes, whisk buttermilk, butter, and egg in a large bowl. Stir in 1 cup of pancake mix. (This amount makes enough for 3 to 4 people.) Cook pancakes on a hot, greased griddle or in a large skillet.

Banana walnut waffles

I've adapted a thicker pancake recipe into waffles here to replace the commercial freezer waffles my kids used to like and to use up overly browned bananas. Bananas travel to Maine via the cold chain, an uninterrupted series of temperature-controlled storage and distribution systems that bring foods from far away safely to my kitchen, so it's paramount not to waste them.

Makes 8 waffles

2 cups all-purpose flour

2 tablespoons sugar

1 tablespoon baking powder

½ teaspoon kosher salt

1¼ cups buttermilk

3 tablespoons melted butter (plus more to grease the waffle iron)

1 ripe banana, mashed

1 teaspoon vanilla extract

¼ cup finely chopped, toasted walnuts

Sliced banana and maple syrup for serving

Whisk the flour, sugar, baking powder, and salt in a large bowl. In a medium-sized mixing bowl, vigorously whisk buttermilk, butter, banana, and vanilla. Pour the wet ingredients into the dry ingredients and mix until batter is smooth. Stir in walnuts. Allow the batter to rest for a few minutes while preheating the waffle iron.

Grease the waffle iron. Ladle batter into the iron based on manufacturer's instructions. Cook waffles until golden brown (time will vary based on your iron). Serve the waffles with sliced bananas and maple syrup.

Grilled lemon thyme buttermilk biscuits with strawberries and cream

You can bake these biscuits in a 400° oven for 12 minutes without oiling or flipping them, but by the time local strawberries are available in Maine, I'd rather be sitting on the patio grilling than standing in the kitchen with a hot oven.

Serves 6

- ½ cup granulated sugar
- 1 tablespoon finely grated lemon zest
- 2 teaspoons finely minced fresh thyme leaves
- 1 quart fresh strawberries, hulled and sliced
- 2 tablespoons fresh lemon juice
- 2¼ cups all-purpose flour, more for kneading
- 1½ teaspoons baking powder
- 1 teaspoon baking soda
- ¼ teaspoon kosher salt
- 6 tablespoons chilled unsalted butter, cut into ⅓-inch cubes
- ⅔ cup chilled buttermilk
- 1 tablespoon neutral, high heat oil such as canola or grapeseed
- 1 to 1½ cups sweetened whipped cream

In a large bowl, combine sugar, zest, and thyme. In a second non-reactive bowl, combine half of the sugar mixture with the strawberries and lemon juice. Set the berries aside to macerate for an hour.

Use a wire brush to thoroughly clean grill grates. Light the grill and close the lid to preheat it to 400°.

Into the bowl with the remaining sugar mixture, whisk flour, baking powder, baking soda, and salt. Add butter pieces and rub them into flour with your fingertips until mixture resembles coarse meal. Add buttermilk and stir with fork just until blended (dough will be sticky). Dump dough onto lightly floured work surface. Knead gently until dough just comes together. Pat dough out to ¾-inch thick circle.

Using a 3-inch-diameter cookie cutter dipped in flour, cut out dough rounds. Gather dough scraps and gently pat out to ¾-inch thickness. Cut out additional rounds. You should have six in total.

Transfer dough rounds to a plate and brush the tops lightly with oil. Check the grill to make sure the temperature is holding steady at 400°. Adjust flow accordingly.

Place biscuits oiled side down directly on grill grates. Lower the lid, and bake until the underside of the biscuits are well marked (5 to 7 minutes). Flip the biscuits, close lid, and cook until the biscuits are golden and a tester inserted in the middle comes out clean (9 to 10 minutes). Remove the biscuits from grill. Cool slightly, slice in half, and serve with sugared berries and cream.

Waste-free raspberry crumb muffins

I found my favorite muffin recipe in the Sarabeth's Bakery Cookbook. *I've adapted the recipe to be a bit more green by making sure it works with all-purpose flour, cutting back on fat and sugar, substituting buttermilk for her milk and orange juice combination, increasing the yield to shrink the gargantuan size, and nipping and tucking processes to eliminate kitchen gadget overload and unnecessary dishes.*

Makes 12 muffins

Streusel:

- 6 tablespoons all-purpose flour
- 2½ tablespoons butter, melted
- 2 tablespoons brown sugar
- ¼ teaspoon vanilla extract
- ⅛ teaspoon cinnamon

Muffins:

- ½ cup neutral oil, such as grapeseed or canola
- ⅔ cups buttermilk
- 2 eggs, at room temperature
- 1 teaspoon orange zest
- 2 cups all-purpose flour
- ½ cup packed light brown sugar
- 1 tablespoon baking powder
- ¼ teaspoon kosher salt
- 1 cup fresh or frozen raspberries

To make the streusel, combine all ingredients in a small bowl. Set aside.

To make the muffins, position a rack in the middle of the oven and preheat to 400°. Line a 12-cup muffin tin or use spent butter wrappers to grease each cup.

Combine oil, buttermilk, eggs, and zest in a large measuring cup. Whisk flour, sugar, baking powder, and salt in a medium bowl. Mix wet and dry ingredients until just combined. Fold in raspberries.

Divide batter among prepared cups. Divvy up the streusel among the muffins. Bake for 10 minutes. Reduce heat to 375°. Bake until tops are golden and a tester inserted in the center of a muffin comes out clean (15 to 18 minutes, longer if you use frozen berries). Cool in the pan for 10 minutes. Remove from the pan to cool completely.

Custardy sweet corn spoon bread

Spoon bread tastes like corn bread but is creamy enough to require a spoon to eat.

Serves 6 to 8
+ Plan-over corncobs for Corn and Clam Chowder, 48

1 cup all-purpose flour

¾ cup stone ground cornmeal

2 teaspoons baking powder

½ teaspoon baking soda

¼ teaspoon ground nutmeg

½ teaspoon kosher salt

3 eggs

1 cup buttermilk

1 cup whole milk

3 tablespoons melted unsalted butter, divided

2 tablespoons honey

2 cups fresh corn kernels (from about 3 cobs)

¼ cup chopped chives

1 cup heavy cream

Preheat oven to 350°. Place a 10- or 12-inch cast iron pan into the oven on the middle rack. Mix the dry ingredients in a large bowl and set aside.

In a separate mixing bowl, whisk eggs, buttermilk, whole milk, 2 tablespoons melted butter, and honey. Add wet ingredients to the dry ones and stir until the batter just comes together. Fold in corn kernels and chives.

Remove skillet from the oven and add 1 tablespoon melted butter. Swirl butter around pan. Slowly pour batter into the pan. Slowly pour cream over the batter but do not mix it in. Bake until top layer is golden brown and a knife inserted into the center comes out clean (35 to 45 minutes). Remove from oven and let stand for 10 minutes before serving.

Maple blueberry self-saucing cake

This slightly sweetened cake sits on top of a maple-blueberry pudding so it's like having two desserts in one. Add ice cream on top for a trifecta. Grill-baking this cake means you don't have to turn on the oven when the blueberries are at their peak. If it's winter, the recipe will also work with frozen berries and can be baked in a 400° oven.

Serves 6 to 8

2 cups blueberries, fresh or frozen

1 cup dark maple syrup

⅔ cup heavy cream

Kosher salt

1 teaspoon lemon zest

½ cup buttermilk

½ cup unsalted butter, melted

1 egg

1 teaspoon vanilla extract

⅔ cup all-purpose flour

⅓ cup whole wheat flour

⅓ cup finely ground cornmeal

1½ teaspoons baking powder

3 tablespoons sugar

½ teaspoon ground cinnamon

Vanilla ice cream, to serve

Fire up the grill. Use a wire brush to clean its grates. If you have a three-burner gas grill, do not light the center element. If you are using a two-burner gas grill or a charcoal one, concentrate the heat to one side. To further diffuse heat, place a baking sheet across grates.

Combine the berries, syrup, cream, and a pinch of salt in a saucepan. Place the pan on the grill and stir the mixture as it comes to a boil. Let the mixture boil for 1 minute. Remove the pan from the heat and stir in the zest. Set aside.

Cover grill to bring its temperature too 400°.

In a large measuring cup, whisk buttermilk, butter, egg, and vanilla. In a large bowl, whisk flours, cornmeal, baking powder, sugar, and cinnamon. Add wet ingredients to dry ones and mix until the batter just comes together.

Pour the berry mixture into an 8- or 9-inch square pan. Dollop the batter on top of the berry mixture. Place the pan on top of the baking sheet set over grill grates. Replace grill cover. Grill-bake cake until the top is golden and the berry mixture bubbles up around sides of the pan (30 to 40 minutes). Let the cake rest for 15 minutes before serving with ice cream.

Christine

Take tea or coffee with heaping spoonful of sustainability

I am always happy to spring forward when Daylight Saving Time begins. I look forward to the pleasure of longer evenings illuminated by natural light, but even so, losing that hour of sleep and waking to darker mornings makes me reach for the biggest teacup in the cupboard.

Given my latitude, neither my tea leaves nor my husband's coffee beans are ever likely to be locally sourced. I prefer Assam tea, which hails from the region of India with the same name. It lies on either side of the Brahmaputra River and is bordered by Bangladesh, Bhutan and Burma (Myanmar). Andy has preferred Columbian coffee since I met him twenty-four years ago, when he was drinking Chock full o'Nuts.

But that's not to say we can't reduce, reuse, and recycle our way to a more sustainable caffeine habit.

Reducing the toll on the humans producing coffee and tea and their environment starts with your purchasing decisions. Opt for products carrying a Fair Trade label. It's easier to find this certification than it used to be.

Other organizations look at ethical coffee from different angles. Direct Trade is a term used by coffee roasters who buy straight from the growers, cutting out both the traditional middleman buyers and sellers and the organizations that control certifications like Fair Trade.

Rainforest Alliance and Bird Friendly certifications make sure coffee production is not put above environmental concerns. The latter, created by the Smithsonian Migratory Bird Center in Washington, D.C., is the stricter of the two because it requires that producers meet organic certification requirements first, and then meet additional criteria concerning forest shade cover and tree biodiversity in the forests that provide habitat for birds and other wildlife.

Another way to reduce the impact of your caffeine habit on the wider world is to buck the single serving, one-time use packaging schemes. Trade your tea bags for loose tea and a strainer. Or do as Hamburg, Germany did and shun all single-use coffee pods—like those made by Keurig and Nespresso. That city banned coffee pods from public buildings because they contributed to "unnecessary resource consumption and waste generation" and "often contain polluting aluminum."

If you buy your coffee by the cup, use a refillable vessel. If you forgot that at home, let the paper cup go topless and wear a glove instead of using a cardboard sleeve to protect your hands. Silly little steps? Maybe, but taking them puts you in the right environmental frame of mind.

Spent coffee grounds and tea leaves can easily be reused. I know a local coffee house owner who uses brewed grounds in her worm farm. It makes the inhabitants happy and in return they produce the compost that keeps her houseplants happy all winter long. And I know another who dries them out and uses them as a deodorizer, rubbing them into stinky dogs' fur before bathing and using them in the fridge like a box of baking soda.

My budding greenness includes no worms at this juncture, but I do use spent coffee grounds and tea leaves, mixed with equal parts warm water and white vinegar, as a means of erasing scratches in the wood floor and on my dining room table. I grind used coffee grounds with black pepper and salt in a 2:1:1 ratio to make a rub for grilled beef that is both flavorful and tenderizing.

But my favorite use for tea leaves—which tend to still have a lot of flavor left in them after a single steep—is to make cookies (Earl Grey Dipper Biscuits, 32) to dip into my tea as I enjoy the prolonged afternoon light.

Cold-brew affogato with cinnamon-scented ice cream, page 34

Earl Grey dipper biscuits

Distinctively English, Earl Grey is black tea flavored with oil from the rind of a bergamot orange, a citrus fruit that looks and tastes like an orange mixed with lemon and a little grapefruit and lime thrown in. The tea is potent and there is plenty of flavor still left in the leaves after you've steeped a cup. Use the spent leaves to make these cookies.

Makes 24 cookies

2 tablespoons Earl Grey previously steeped tea leaves

⅓ cup organic granulated sugar

1 vanilla bean, split and seeds removed

1 teaspoon finely grated orange zest

¼ teaspoon ground cinnamon

¼ cup confectioners' sugar

1¼ cups all-purpose flour

Pinch of kosher salt

½ cup room temperature butter, cut into pieces

¼ cup heavy cream

½ cup raw sugar

Spread out the tea leaves in a small skillet over medium heat and toast until fragrant (2 to 3 minutes). Toss the toasted leaves into the bowl of a food processor. Cool slightly. Add granulated sugar to the bowl, along with the vanilla bean seeds (stick the pod in your sugar bowl!), and orange zest. Pulse the ingredients together to get a fine, speckled powder. Add the cinnamon, confectioners' sugar, flour, and salt. Pulse again to combine. Add the butter and cream and pulse to form a rough dough.

Spread an 18-inch piece of parchment paper on a flat surface and sprinkle half of the raw sugar around it. Turn dough out onto prepared sheet and shape it into a 9-inch log with a 3-inch diameter. Gently press down on the top of the log so that a cross-section will be more oval than round. This makes the finished cookies better suited for dipping. Sprinkle the remaining ¼ cup raw sugar over the top of the log. Wrap tightly and refrigerate for two hours.

Preheat oven to 350°. Line two baking sheets with silicone mats. Slice chilled dough into ⅓-inch slices and place on prepared sheets, 2 inches apart. Bake until edges begin to brown slightly, (10 to 12 minutes). Cool on pans for 5 minutes and transfer to a wire rack to cool completely.

Cold-brew affogato with cinnamon-scented ice cream

I've swapped out a hot shot of espresso that traditionally gets poured over an elegantly simple scoop of vanilla gelato with 2 ounces of cold-brew coffee. The ice cream gets "drowned" in coffee (the literal meaning of "affogato"), but it doesn't melt as quickly on hot summer nights.

Serves 4

1 pint cinnamon coffee ice cream (recipe opposite)

1 cup cold-brew concentrate

Shaved chocolate or crushed chocolate-covered espresso beans

Scoop the ice cream into 4 pretty bowls. Pour ¼ cup of cold brew over each scoop. Garnish with shaved chocolate or espresso beans. Serve immediately.

Coffee brew tip
Cold-brew coffee concentrate, made by steeping 1 ounce of ground coffee in 12 ounces of cold water in an airtight jar, is sweeter on the tongue and gentler on the stomach because fewer of the coffees bitter acids are activated in the absence of heat.

Cinnamon coffee ice cream

This is a subtly flavored, creamy cold treat. If you don't have the gear to churn it from its custard base into ice cream, skip the affogato (recipe opposite) and pour the mixture, hot or cold, over angel food cake made from leftover egg whites.

Makes 1 quart

2 cups half and half

¾ cup raw sugar

¼ cup whole roasted coffee beans

3 cinnamon sticks, broken to bits

Pinch of kosher salt

1 cup heavy cream

5 large egg yolks

Optional mix in: chopped chocolate covered coffee beans

Heat the half and half, sugar, coffee beans, cinnamon sticks, and salt in a medium saucepan, stirring until the sugar melts. Take care that the mixture does not boil over. Cover, remove from heat, and let steep for 1 hour. Strain mixture, compost the solids, and reheat the liquid over low heat.

Pour heavy cream into a medium sized bowl. Nestle this bowl into a bigger one filled with ice water.

Whisk the egg yolks in a small bowl and gradually add the warm, cinnamon and coffee infused half and half mixture to the yolks. Continue to whisk constantly. Transfer tempered egg yolk mixture back into the saucepan, place over medium heat, and stir constantly until the custard thickens and coats the back of a spoon. Strain the custard into the bowl of cream sitting on ice. Stir the custard until cool, and refrigerate until cold.

Churn custard in an ice cream maker according to manufacturer's instructions. If using chocolate covered coffee beans, add them during the last minute of churning. Serve immediately or store in an airtight container for up to a week.

Husk cherry and hot pepper upside-down cornbread, page 41

Soups, salads & sides

Christine

Kohlrabi butchery is a greener life skill

I saw a kohlrabi bulb as big as my head in the market one day in early June. It triggered flashbacks of force feeding my family gobs of the stuff that came weekly in my first Community Supported Agriculture shares (circa 2009), before my farmer got a handle on the whole crop diversification thing. As I stared at the bulb, my dread resurfaced, and, as though cued by my memory, a fellow shopper wondered aloud how anyone could possibly use a brassica that big.

I gravitate toward extraordinary farmers market items. Bring on the husk cherries (upside-down cornbread, 41), shishito peppers, tatsoi (smoked trout and soba noodle salad, 120), and zucchini blossoms (fried zucchini blossoms, 65)! But three vegetables I've balked at bringing home are kohlrabi of any size, gnarly celery root, and blue-gray, warty Hubbard squash.

I've come to realize, though, that keeping a sharp knife and honing my vegetable butchery technique are necessary skills for a greener life.

On the first day of culinary school, administrators hand you a bundle of shiny new knives. The remainder of the week you cut potatoes—first into rectangles, then ¼-inch sticks (called batonnet), then julienned strips, and finally tiny dice (the fancy French word is brunoise).

A chef measures and weighs your end product, looks into your waste bin, and routinely commands another round of cuts. Some chefs are more tyrannical than others, but the message is consistent and clear: With razor-sharp knives at your disposal, there is no excuse for even a wasted ounce of food.

A sharp knife helps you work quickly and with precision. It damages fewer flavor-containing cells, so food looks and tastes better than it does when crushed by a dull blade. Culinary students learn this lesson to buoy a restaurant's reputation and bottom line, but the green angle applies too. Keeping your knives well-honed cuts down on food waste.

To keep your knives sharp, use them only for their intended purpose and never to cut frozen foods. Also, employ wooden or kitchen-safe plastic cutting boards, wash and dry knives by hand, hone them on a steel once a week, and store them either in a sleeve, on a hanging magnetic strip or in a knife block. These practices will keep your knives sharper longer, saving you time on the sharpening block (or money if you choose to visit a professional sharpener instead).

Now back to the kohlrabi.

The same butchering principles apply as with any other orb-shaped, thick-skinned root vegetable: beets, turnips, rutabagas, and celeriac. You take a thin slice off both the top and bottom of the bulb, rest it on the broadest cut end and, working from top to bottom, follow the curve of the kohlrabi sliding the knife under the skin to remove it. From here you can safely slice, shred or dice the bulb according to your recipe's instructions.

To cook it, you need to know that kohlrabi's flavor profile and how it reacts to heat mirrors its cousins: broccoli, kale, or Brussels sprouts. It can be used shredded raw in slaws, roasted in chunky medleys to bring out its sweetness, and sliced thinly and baked into gratins with ingredients like chives, cumin, curry, dill, garlic, ginger, mustard and/or parsley that round out its peppery flavor.

If you're stumped, you can always turn to green cooks who have already paved the way. My two go-to references are Deborah Madison's *Vegetable Literacy*, and Cara Mangini's *The Vegetable Butcher*. Both explain how to choose seasonal vegetables wisely and store them properly. A kohlrabi should be firm to the touch, heavy for its size, and have crisp, dark green leaves. To store, liberate it of its leaves, which can be used like mustard greens, and it will keep very well in the crisper drawer for as long as 10 days.

Armed with knowledge and a sharp 10-inch chef's knife, the prospect of cooking kohlrabi, celery root, and Hubbard squash becomes a little less scary.

That's a steel!

A honing steel is a rod of ceramic or diamond-coated steel used to realign a knife's edges by running both sides of a blade across it at a 20 degree angle an equal number of times.

Kohlrabi fritters

I adapted this recipe from a Jewish friend's potato latke recipe. She uses a kitchen heirloom (a flat wire grating tool) to shred potatoes and onions to the proper consistency. I suggest a food processor for firmer kohlrabies. For the flour, I use half all-purpose and half local whole wheat or rye. If your kohlrabi came with its leaves attached, shred them and toss them with lemon juice, olive oil, and salt and pepper to serve with the fritters.

Makes 10-12 fritters

Olive oil

Canola oil

2 medium (8 ounces each) white or purple kohlrabies, peeled

1 medium-sized sweet onion (like Vidalia, for example)

1 large egg

½ cup flour

2 tablespoons chopped fresh dill

1 teaspoon baking powder

1 teaspoon dry mustard powder

¼ teaspoon red chili pepper flakes

Flaky sea salt

In a 10-inch frying pan with 2-inch sides, pour oil to a depth of 1 inch, using equal parts olive and canola oils. Heat oil over medium-high heat to 350-375°.

Cut the kohlrabi into chunks. Using a food processor with a grating disc shred the chunks and the onion. (A box grater is greener, but it will take more time and effort.) Transfer to a large bowl and add egg, flour, dill, baking powder, mustard and chili flakes. Mix thoroughly.

When the oil is hot (it should sizzle wildly when you drop a single kohlrabi shred into it), take about 2 tablespoons of batter in your hand and flatten it into a 2- to 2½-inch round, and carefully slide it into oil. Three or four fritters should fit in the pan at once. Turn fritters when the bottom sides are golden brown (2 to 3 minutes) and cook until the second side is golden brown. Transfer cooked fritters to drain on a recycled paper bag, immediately sprinkling each with sea salt. Repeat process until all batter is used. These fritters are best served immediately, but you can hold them for up to an hour in a 200° oven.

NOTE: Cool and strain the fry oil for future use. Store it in the refrigerator for up to three weeks.

Husk cherry and hot pepper upside-down cornbread

The husk cherries, hot and not-so-hot peppers, brown sugar, and butter add texture and flavor to an otherwise run-of-the-mill cornbread that's turned on its head.

Serves 6 to 8

1½ pints husk cherries (about 1½ cups of cherries, husked)

1 jalapeño pepper

1 poblano pepper

½ cup unsalted butter, melted

⅔ cup light brown sugar

1 cup stone-ground cornmeal

1 cup all-purpose flour

2½ teaspoons baking powder

½ teaspoon kosher salt

¼ teaspoon baking soda

1¼ cups buttermilk

2 eggs

1 cup fresh or frozen corn kernels

Preheat oven to 400°.

Remove the husks from the husk cherries and cut half the berries in half. Leave the remaining berries whole. Slice peppers into ¼-inch rounds.

Place a 12-inch cast iron skillet over medium heat, add 4 tablespoons melted butter, all the husk cherries, pepper slices, and ⅓ cup of brown sugar. Cook, stirring until the sugar melts and the cherries start to break down slightly (3 to 4 minutes). Remove pan from heat and set aside.

Whisk remaining ⅓ cup brown sugar, cornmeal, flour, baking powder, salt, and baking soda in a large bowl. In a large measuring cup, whisk buttermilk, eggs, and remaining 4 tablespoons butter. Stir wet ingredients into dry ones until just combined. Fold in corn kernels.

Gently pour batter into cast-iron pan, over the husk cherries and peppers. Bake until a toothpick inserted into center of cornbread comes out clean (20 to 24 minutes). Remove pan from oven. Place a plate larger than the circumference of the pan over it, and flip the cornbread to reveal the caramelized ground cherry and pepper top.

Serve warm or at room temperature.

Kimchi ramen

Remember the cabbage soup diet of the 1950s? Or when it came back in the late 80s? That was bland and slimy. This is nothing like it.

Serves 2

4 cups vegetable broth

½ cup sweet onion slices

¼ cup shredded apple

¼ cup sliced shallots

½ lime, thinly sliced

1-inch piece of fresh ginger, peeled and thinly sliced

5 garlic cloves, peeled thinly sliced

½ to 1 cup kimchi, depending on its heat

3 tablespoons white miso

2 cups cooked ramen or soba noodles

1 cup shaved cabbage

½ cup sliced scallions (green parts only)

2 tablespoons neutral oil

2 eggs

Combine broth, onions, apples, shallots, lime, ginger, garlic, and kimchi in a medium saucepan and simmer for 30 minutes. Stir in miso and keep warm over very low heat.

Divide cooked noodles, fresh cabbage, and scallions between two bowls. Heat oil in a skillet over medium heat, crack the eggs into it, and fry eggs to desired doneness.

Pour 2 cups of hot broth through a strainer over noodles into each bowl and top each with a fried egg.

Caramelized ginger parsnips

This recipe is modeled after one given to me by my knife sharpener's wife. She deftly cuts sweet winter parsnips into shapes her grandchildren think are French fries. I finish this dish with Garbage Finishing Salts (186) made from dried carrot and ginger peels that would have otherwise gone into the compost bin.

Serves 4

+ Plan-over parsnips for Harvest Mason Jar Salad with Grains and Greens, 73

2 pounds parsnips, peeled with ends trimmed

4 tablespoons unsalted butter

¼ teaspoon ground ginger

Garbage Finishing Salt (186)

Cut peeled parsnips into sticks the size of large French fries. Lay parsnips on a dry towel and wrap tightly. Melt the butter in a large skillet over medium heat and add parsnips, tossing to coat. Sprinkle with ground ginger. Cover the skillet tightly. Cook over medium heat until parsnips are golden brown (10 to 12 minutes). Add 2 tablespoons water, replace cover, and steam until the water has evaporated and parsnips are golden, tender and caramelized.

Season with finishing salt if you have it, plain kosher salt, and pepper, if you don't. Serve half and store half in an air-tight container in the refrigerator for up to three days.

Date night fennel and celery salad

Fennel is an ideal date night food because, according to the Oxford Companion to Italian Food, *it both calms flatulence and sweetens breath. In this dish, fennel (bulb, fronds, and seeds) romances celery (stalks and leaves).*

Serves 2 (of course!)

1 fennel bulb, plus a few of its fronds (chopped)

6 stalks of celery, plus ¼ cup celery leaves

½ cup chopped, toasted hazelnuts

2 tablespoons chopped fresh tarragon leaves

2 tablespoons olive oil

2 teaspoons maple syrup

1 teaspoon lemon zest plus 1 tablespoon lemon juice

½ teaspoon fennel seeds, toasted and coarsely ground

½ teaspoon sea salt

¼ teaspoon cracked black pepper

⅛ teaspoon celery seed

½ ounce shaved hard, salty cheese (such as Parmesan, Asiago, or an aged local cheddar)

Slice both fennel bulb and celery stalks as thinly as possible and toss with fennel fronds, celery leaves, hazelnuts and tarragon in a bowl. Add olive oil, maple syrup, lemon zest and juice, fennel seeds, salt, pepper, and celery seed. Toss well. Transfer to a serving platter. Scatter cheese over salad and serve immediately.

Grow it

Both fennel and celery can be regrown by sticking their joined root ends in water and giving them a little sunshine.

Apple, carrot, and kale slaw

This is my go-to picnic slaw because it comes together quickly, is made with readily available ingredients, and stays crisp on the buffet line. Lacinato kale, also called dinosaur kale due to its rough, scaly feel, is best in this recipe because its flatter shape means it's easier to cut into strips.

Serves 4 generously
+ Plan-over vegetables for Shrimp and Shredded Kale, Fennel, and Carrot Stir-fry, 118

2 bunch Lacinato kale, cut into julienne strips

3 cups shredded carrots

6 scallions, trimmed and thinly sliced

1 teaspoon minced fresh jalapeno pepper

2 cups julienned Gala, Cortland, Empire or Fuji apples (skin-on)

¾ cup Sweet and Sour Slaw Dressing (172)

2 tablespoons chopped cilantro leaves

In a large bowl, combine vegetables. Remove half and store in an airtight container in the refrigerator to make Shrimp and Shredded Kale, Fennel, and Carrot Stir-fry (118).

Add apples. Pour dressing over slaw. Toss to mix and let stand for at least 15 minutes or up to 2 hours before serving. Sprinkle cilantro over finished slaw.

Christine

Sustainable stone soup

Food waste is a staggering problem in the United States. The government estimates that between 30 and 40 percent of all the food flowing into our supply chain gets thrown out. The land, water, labor and energy used in producing, processing, transporting, preparing, and storing that food are wasted as well. Wholesome food (food that could have fed our hungry families) is the single largest substance going into our municipal landfills.

As kids, we were told to finish the food on our plates. As adults, it seems we need a reminder to use up the food in our cupboards and fridges before it goes bad.

My mom used to hold a soup and bread open house in the middle of winter when it had been too long since anyone had seen anyone else walking around the neighborhood. She'd invite her whole world and ask them to bring either a pot of soup, a loaf of bread, or a dessert to share. She never wanted anyone to dig deep into their pockets to make their contribution, but rather encouraged folks to dig deep into their pantries, into the backs of their refrigerators and into the corners of their cabinets to bring what they had on hand.

I recently revived her tradition by hosting my own Sustainable Stone Soup potluck supper. We veered a bit from the basic theme of the old folk tale. We didn't seed our soup with a stone but from the forgotten recesses of our larders. Neither was there any manipulation of the local townspeople as fifty folks of all ages came, bringing 11 soups, many loaves, and a half dozen desserts.

Selections ranged from Roasted Farmers Market Seconds Soup (49) to a curried pantry soup whose creator admitted she could not reproduce it as it was made from bits and bobs she'll not likely have on hand in similar quantities ever again. There was a shrub (sweetened drinking vinegar) made from USDA surplus cherries, a crisp made with the last of the peaches from a tree growing in a friend's yard, and rolls leftover from dinner the night before.

The party was still a party, for sure, but the creative ways in which contributors dug deep into their cupboards and vegetable drawers and tapped their imaginations and cooking skills to make dishes instead of trash, proved to be useful as both conversation starters and lessons learned.

Chicken stock
Ten black peppercorns, 8 parsley stems, 6 sprigs of thyme, 4 cups of chicken bones, 2 cups of vegetable trimmings, and 1 gallon of water simmered for 4 hours makes 3 quarts of stock. Generally, stock refers to liquid made from simmering meat bones and broth is liquid made from simmering meat and or vegetables.

Parmigiano-reggiano broth with ravioli

Every wedge of real Parmigiano-Reggiano—cut from 80-pound wheels imported from the Emilia-Romagna region of central Italy—should comprise 10 percent rind. The rind, which is stamped repeatedly with the cheese's name, helps cut pieces stay fresh. Since this cheese sells for $17 to $25 per pound, it's only sensible to use every last bit, including the rind. Store the rinds in the cheese drawer of the refrigerator in an air-tight bag until you've accumulated enough to make this broth.

Serves 4
+ Plan-over 4 cups of broth

6 (3- to 4-inch) pieces of Parmigiano-Reggiano rind, trimmed of any moldy bits

6 large garlic cloves, thinly sliced

4 sprigs thyme

6 sprigs parsley, leaves removed, chopped and set aside

2 tablespoons extra-virgin olive oil

Sea salt and freshly ground black pepper

1 pound fresh or frozen ravioli (or tortellini)

¼ cup freshly grated Parmigiano-Reggiano cheese

Combine rinds, garlic, thyme, parsley, oil, and 10 cups of cold water in a 6-quart pot. Simmer gently over medium heat, partially covered, for 30 minutes. Taste the broth. If you would like a richer broth, keep simmering. When you like the flavor, remove pan from heat and strain the broth. Compost herbs, but cool and save the rinds, which can be used once more to flavor another soup. Season broth to taste with salt and pepper.

Remove 4 cups from the pot, cool and refrigerate for another use.

When ready to serve, bring broth to a boil. Drop in ravioli or tortellini. When the pasta floats, remove the pot from the heat.

Divide pasta among four warm bowls. Pour 1½ cups broth into each bowl. Sprinkle each with grated cheese and reserved chopped parsley. Serve immediately.

Corn and clam chowder

Try this chowder in summer when corn is fresh. If you've got more corn than you can eat in August, remove kernels from the cobs, make a big pot of corn broth, freeze both broth and corn, and enjoy this dish year round.

Serves 4
+ Plan-over 4 cups of corn broth

5 ears of fresh corn, shucked

2 large stems of fresh parsley

2 large stems of fresh thyme

8 black peppercorns

1 bay leaf

1 tablespoon olive oil

1 tablespoon butter

4 ounces of chopped, smoky bacon

1 medium sweet onion, chopped

1 large russet potato, scrubbed and cut into ½-inch cubes

1 cup bottled clam juice (or seafood stock in a pinch)

1 teaspoon salt

½ teaspoon black pepper

2 cups of cooked chopped clams

24 fresh whole clams (hard or soft shell as you like), soaked and scrubbed

1 cup cream or half and half

Corn broth:

Remove the kernels from cobs and the leaves from both parsley and thyme stems. Set aside the kernels and herb leaves. Put cobs, parsley, and thyme stems, peppercorns, and bay leaf into a pot with 10 cups of cold water. Bring to a boil over high heat. Reduce heat to medium and simmer for 1½ hours. Strain, compost solids, and refrigerate or freeze broth in two, four-cup portions until ready to use.

Chowder:

Heat olive oil and butter in a 6-quart pot over medium heat until butter foams. Add bacon and cook for 3 minutes to render some of the fat. Add onion and sauté until translucent (4-6 minutes). Add potatoes and corn kernels and cook for 2 minutes. Add clam juice, 4 cups of corn broth, and salt and pepper. Simmer until potatoes are tender (6 to 8 minutes). Add chopped and whole clams, cover and cook until clams open (4 to 5 minutes). Check broth for seasoning. Stir in cream. Serve immediately.

Corn kernel catcher
A Bundt cake pan can double as a corn kernel catcher. Push a husked piece of corn, pointy end down, into the tube. Run a sharp knife down the sides of the cob, turning as you go and the pan neatly catches all of the kernels.

Roasted farmers market seconds soup

Farmers market seconds are scraggly looking, extra-ripe, maybe slightly bruised produce that doesn't quite make the retail grade, but is still absolutely edible, perfect for things like jam and sauce, and sold at a good discount. If they don't have a bin of seconds out on display, just ask your farmer or produce aisle clerk! This recipe is adaptable to whichever seconds you can get your hands on. Because you chop and roast these fruits and vegetables to intensify their flavors, and puree them to a pulp to finish the soup, they needn't be picture perfect before going into the pot.

Makes 2 quarts of soup
+ Plan-over roasted vegetables for Harvest Mason Jar Salad with Grains and Greens, 73

6 cups peeled, cored, and chopped farmers market seconds (carrots, corn, parsnips, pumpkin, sweet potato, or winter squash)

¼ cup olive oil

Kosher salt and ground black pepper

1 medium sweet onion (such as Vidalia), peeled and chopped

2 large garlic cloves, peeled and roughly chopped

4 to 5 cups corn broth (Plan-over from Corn and Clam Chowder, 48)

3 large sprigs fresh thyme, plus 1 teaspoon leaves for garnish

Yogurt, sour cream, or crème fraîche for garnish

Roasted corn kernels for garnish (optional)

Preheat oven to 400°.

Place cut vegetables on a rimmed baking sheet, toss with 2 tablespoons of olive oil, spread into a single layer on the sheet, and sprinkle generously with salt. If you are using different types of vegetables in combination, it's best to roast them on separate pans as roasting times may vary. Roast until the vegetables are soft (25 to 45 minutes, depending on the vegetable) turning with a spatula twice so they get caramelized on all sides. Reserve half of the roasted vegetables for Harvest Mason Jar Salad with Grains and Greens (73).

Meanwhile, cook onion in remaining 2 tablespoons olive oil in a large pot until translucent (3 to 5 minutes). Add garlic and cook for 1 minute. Add broth or water and toss in thyme sprigs. Simmer for 10 minutes. Add the remaining roasted vegetables and any juices that may have accumulated in the pan, and simmer for 10 more minutes. Fish out thyme sprigs (the leaves should have fallen off in the cooking process). Puree the soup until smooth, adding a little more broth or water if it seems thick. Add salt and pepper to taste. Serve hot, garnished with thyme leaves, a dollop of the dairy product of your choice, and corn kernels.

Christine

When your eyes were too big for your belly

I have a hard time staying within my food budget. Farmers market wooden tokens and portable credit card machines just make that more difficult. As market stalls overflow with gorgeous produce, I want it all: each type of slicing tomato, every bouquet of herbs, all the lovely heads of lettuce, yellow, green, and purple beans, peak of summer corn, experimental melons, bright berries by the quart, radishes and baby turnips in all sizes, and chili peppers running up and down the Scoville scale.

You see my problem? As recently as five years ago, I was kept in check by the cash in my wallet, as credit cards were useless at farmers markets. But electronic payment systems have enabled my eyes to become bigger than my family's collective stomach on any given market day. Rather than heeding my husband's fiscal warnings to buy only what we can eat until the next market day, I have developed four kitchen behaviors to make sure none of my extraneous produce purchases go to waste.

First, I take the time on market day to prep produce for longer-term storage. Herbs look artfully trendy sitting in a mason jar on the counter but they will last much longer if you wrap them loosely in a clean flour-sack towel and store them in the front of the vegetable crisper. Don't wash herbs until just before you want to use them, as water will hurry decomposition. On the other hand, lovely lettuces should get washed, torn into pieces and twirled in the salad spinner before they are wrapped and stored for easy salad pickings.

For heartier greens like kale and chard, and edible leaves that come attached to any root vegetables, I advise removing the leaves from their stems in bite-sized pieces (save the stems for green smoothies or to be chopped and sautéed). Wash and spin them dry and place them front and center in the refrigerator so that every time you open the door, your mind registers the sub-conscious message of "USE ME"!

Second, I make sure eggplant, bell peppers, summer squash, and zucchini get eaten throughout the week by grilling them en masse on market day. Firing up the grill just once conserves energy, and having vegetables already cooked means they can easily be included in lunchtime sandwiches and quick dinners.

Third, I store the majority of my fruit on the counter so that it ripens to peak flavor. When it's in plain sight, it gets eaten before the snack drawer gets tapped.

And finally, I put up a few jars of preserved fruits or veggies. For many people, preserving summer bounty conjures up long, hot days in a steamy kitchen preserving gobs of stuff. But it doesn't have to be that big of a production. Three jars of pickled beets or dilly beans takes fewer than 45 minutes to pull off and are just as welcome on a gray February day as any big batch jar would be.

To fridge or not to fridge?

Yes: Asparagus, berries, broccoli, Brussels sprouts, cabbage, carrots, cauliflower, celery, citrus, corn, herbs, ginger, greens, lettuce, mushrooms, peppers, summer squash. No: apples, avocados, bananas, cucumber, eggplant, garlic, honey, melons, pears, onions, potatoes, stone fruit, tomatoes, winter squash.

Plan-over fingerling potatoes

The Irish side of me always wants potatoes on the plate. Here is a recipe—or three, really—for how I serve them so none of the beautiful fingerlings I buy locally get wasted. For the first meal, we eat them dressed in a lemon vinaigrette, for the second, smashed and oven-crisped with rosemary olive oil, and for the third, sliced and sautéed with scallions.

Serves 4
+ Plan-over 2 side dishes

3 pounds fingerling potatoes, scrubbed

⅓ cup apple cider vinegar

⅓ cup kosher salt, plus more for seasoning

Zest of 1 lemon and
3 tablespoons juice

2 small garlic cloves

1 teaspoon Dijon mustard

1 teaspoon white wine vinegar

1 cup olive oil

Black pepper

2 teaspoons of chopped fresh cilantro, basil, or marjoram (or a mix)

1 sprig rosemary

1 red bell pepper, diced

½ teaspoon chipotle chili powder

6 scallions, green parts only, sliced thinly on a diagonal

Combine potatoes, cider vinegar, ⅓ cup salt and 1½ gallons of water in a large pot. Place pot over high heat until it boils. Reduce heat to medium and simmer until potatoes are tender (10-12 minutes). The timing will depend on the size of the potatoes; check for tenderness with the tip of a knife.

Drain potatoes and let them sit in the colander for 10 minutes until they are cool enough to handle. Slice ⅓ of cooked potatoes in half lengthwise and place them in a large bowl. Spread remaining ⅔ potatoes on a baking sheet to cool completely. Refrigerate for future use.

Combine lemon zest and juice, 1 garlic clove, mustard, white wine vinegar, and ½ cup olive oil in a blender and blend until the vinaigrette is emulsified.

Pour over warm potatoes and toss. Sprinkle with pepper and chopped herbs and serve warm.

Fingerling Plan-over 1: Bring half of the remaining potatoes to room temperature. Use a small saucepan to heat ⅓ cup olive oil, 1 garlic clove and rosemary sprig. When the oil simmers slightly, remove it from the heat and let sit for 15 minutes. Preheat oven to 425°. Line a baking sheet with a silicone mat. Spread the potatoes around lined pan. Use a flat-bottom coffee cup to smoosh each potato so the skin cracks and the potato flattens to about ½-inch. Pour flavored oil over potatoes. Sprinkle liberally with salt and black pepper. Bake until crispy (25 to 30 minutes).

Fingerling Plan-over 2: Slice the remaining fingerlings into ¼-inch coins. Heat 2 tablespoons olive oil in a large skillet over medium-high heat. Add red peppers and sauté for 3 minutes. Add chili powder and potatoes and sauté, stirring frequently, until the potatoes start to brown (10 to 12 minutes). Remove from heat, toss potatoes with scallions. Serve warm.

Kale rabe and potato tart

The only real rabe is broccoli rabe. Called rapini in Italy, all of this green cruciferous vegetable's parts—leaves, buds (which resemble tiny broccoli spears), and stems—are deliciously edible. Recently, spicy mustard greens and kale have been marketed with the same surname. After these plants have produced leafy greens in high tunnels all winter long, warmer weather forces them to start to go to seed and resemble rabe. The flavor is a more bitter kale or spicier mustard greens, so blanch them in salted, boiling water before sautéing. If rabe is not on offer, try this recipe with any other hearty leafy green in equal measure.

Serves 6 to 8

1½ pounds potatoes, scrubbed and sliced in ⅛-inch rounds

1 bunch (about ¾-pound) kale or spicy mustard rabe

Kosher salt

1 yellow onion, diced

2 tablespoons olive oil

2 cloves garlic, minced

½ to 1 teaspoon red chili pepper flakes

3 eggs, lightly beaten

¾ cup heavy cream

4 ounces cheddar cheese, shredded

Dough for 1 savory pie crust

Preheat oven to 350°.

Place the potato rounds in cold, salted water and bring to a boil over medium-high heat. Reduce heat to medium and simmer potatoes until they are fork tender (6 to 8 minutes). Use a slotted spoon to remove potatoes from the water and spread them on a towel to dry.

Turn heat to high and bring water back to a rolling boil. Remove and compost the tough ends of kale or mustard rabe. Roughly chop rabe and blanch it in boiling water until tender (3-5 minutes). Drain and submerge rabe in a bowl of cold water, drain again, and squeeze out excess water.

In a medium-sized skillet, sauté the onions in olive oil over medium heat until translucent (4 to 6 minutes). Add garlic and chili pepper flakes and sauté 1 minute longer. Add kale and ½ teaspoon salt and stir.

Roll out the pie crust and fit it into a 10-inch tart pan.

Combine the vegetable mixture with beaten eggs, cream, and half of the cheese.

Arrange half of the potato rounds in a single layer over crust. Sprinkle potatoes with ¼ teaspoon salt. Spread ¾ of kale rabe mixture over potatoes. Repeat potato, salt, and kale layers and sprinkle the remainder of cheese on top.

Bake until tart is golden brown on top and eggs are completely set (40 to 45 minutes). Remove from oven and cool slightly before attempting to cut the tart. Serve warm or at room temperature.

Day-old bread and mozzarella salad

This recipe is halfway between two Italian summertime staples: Panzanella, made with stale bread, and caprese, made with basil, tomato, and mozzarella.

Serves 4 to 6
+ Plan-over 1 cup of breadcrumbs for Orrechiette with Cauliflower, Pancetta, and Breadcrumbs, 100

¼ cup extra-virgin olive oil

8 slices of day-old crusty bread, cut into 1-inch cubes

Sea salt and freshly ground pepper, to taste

1 large, ripe beefsteak tomato

1 teaspoon grated garlic

3 tablespoons minced basil flowers (optional)

1 tablespoon red-wine vinegar

1 pint of cherry or grape tomatoes, halved

1 (8-ounce) ball of fresh mozzarella, torn into 2-inch pieces

½ cup torn basil leaves

¼ cup slivered shallot

Heat 2 tablespoons of oil in a skillet over high heat. Toss in the bread and stir until all sides are toasted. Remove pan from heat, season croutons with salt and pepper, and cool. Once cooled, grind half of the croutons in a food processor for Plan-over bread crumbs for Orrechiette with Cauliflower, Pancetta, and Breadcrumbs (100).

Squeeze the tomato seeds and their gel through a fine mesh sieve placed over a large bowl. Use a rubber spatula to push gel through sieve, and compost seeds. Grate the cut sides of the tomatoes on the large holes of a boxed grater into bowl. Compost tomato skins.

Stir garlic, optional basil flowers, and vinegar into grated tomato mixture. Whisk in 2 tablespoons olive oil. Add halved tomatoes, cheese, toasted bread, torn basil leaves, and shallot. Toss gently. Season with salt and pepper to taste. Serve at room temperature.

Christine

Use your freezer as a green eating vending machine

Think of your freezer as a green eating vending machine. Freezing is the easiest way to preserve local foods at the season's peak, gives protective shelter to leftovers waiting to be eaten, and significantly cuts down on the number of times we all have to run out to get dinner.

That said, I think we can all admit that this has happened to us: You tiptoe into the kitchen for a late-night dip into the ice cream but when you open the freezer door, a brick of mystery food covered in ice crystals falls out onto your foot, shattering the moment, the corner of the brick's container, and a couple of metatarsals.

This late night disaster proves many of us are doing the freezer thing all wrong.

Done right, the freezer is the food-waste warrior's best friend, says Dana Gunders, staff scientist with the Natural Resources Defense Council, who I turn to for many waste management tips. She says the friendship has to be maintained with proper prep, packaging, and planned usage.

For food destined for the freezer, know how long it might be in there. If it's only a few days, a tight wrap in freezer paper will do the job. Blanch vegetables to prepare them for a longer stay. This will stop destructive enzymes, protect their texture, and yield higher quality, more nutritious beans and peas when you do eat them.

Meats should be removed from store packaging, trimmed of excessive fat, wrapped tightly in plastic wrap and then in aluminum foil to avoid freezer burn.

Moist items (like berries, corn kernels, or portioned cookie dough) should be spread out on a tray to freeze individually and then bagged for storage. Watery items (like melons) should be pureed before freezing.

Use clear, airtight containers that come in or can be formed into stackable shapes. Divide food into portions you'll use in one meal. Gunders suggests slicing loaves of bread, forming ground meat into patties and freezing soup portions in muffin tins before bagging them. All containers should be nearly full to help prevent ice crystals from forming.

From a green point of view, this seems like a lot of plastic. But you can use glass canning jars if that is a problem for you. Since all foods expand in the freezer, each glass jar should have a ½ inch space left at the top to allow for that.

A freezer should be packed to allow for both airflow and organization. Items should be stacked tightly but not shoehorned into every available space. Food intended for freezing should be added gradually. The National Center for Home Preservation says not to add more than 3 pounds of food per cubic foot of freezer space in a 24-hour period.

Every package should be clearly marked with its contents and the date. Alternatively, you can establish signature containers for certain items. For example, 2-cup containers with blue tops hold the kids' carrot soup and 1-cup ones with red tops hold the Sungold tomato soup you keep for yourself. Also, smaller snack bag bundles of things like garden peas can be stored unlabeled in a larger container and labeled just once.

Post a white board on the outside of the freezer listing what it contains to save both time spent by the eater in search of food and energy for the appliance working hard to keep its internal temperature constant.

Ice cube trays

Pour freezable liquids (coffee, tea, stock, wine, egg whites, or fruit juice) into trays rather than down the drain. Once they are frozen solid in these tablespoon portions, store the cubes in labeled bags, and pull them out when you need their flavor in your recipes.

Slow-roasted tomatoes

I serve a third of this recipe with bread (most times I don't share); a third stuffed in mushrooms with a melted washed rind cheese like Taleggio; and, a third tossed with a pound of hot pasta, 1/4 cup of goat cheese and chopped olive oil-cured black olives. The base recipe for these tomatoes is adaptable to the number you can get your hands on and the number of racks you can fit into your oven. To freeze them, cool them completely, layer one cup of tomatoes in a stackable container and drizzle 1/4 cup of the roasting oil over them.

Serves 4
+ Plan-over stuffed mushrooms and pasta

3 quarts of smallish plum or big cherry tomatoes, halved with seeds removed

9 cloves of garlic, peeled and cut into thin slices

3 tablespoons fresh thyme leaves

Zest of 1 lemon

Kosher salt

Freshly ground pepper

¾ cup olive oil

Preheat oven to 300°. Line two baking sheets with tin foil. Lay tomatoes, cut side up, on the trays, leaving a bit of room between them. Place a sliver of garlic in each tomato. Sprinkle thyme, lemon zest, salt, and pepper liberally over tomatoes. Pour olive oil over tomatoes. Slide pan into oven, close door, and reduce heat to 275°. Roast until tomatoes are collapsed and a bit darkened around the edges (75 to 90 minutes).

Frozen plum tomatoes
I can can tomatoes. But I'd rather freeze them. Remove cores with a melon baller. Freeze them whole, spread out on a tray. Plunk them in an airtight container when frozen. Use them at will; the peels slide off as they thaw.

Lobster and corn wontons with shredded vegetables and spicy corn broth

There is really no point in making only a few of the wontons in a package of 50. You make dozens and freeze what you aren't going to eat straight away. To freeze, simply lay them out on a sheet pan before putting them in the freezer and once they are frozen, transfer them to a container. To cook them from frozen, just simmer them 2 to 3 minutes longer than if they were fresh.

Makes 4 bowls of soup
+ Plan-over 30 wontons to freeze

Wontons:

¾ pound cooked lobster meat

2 teaspoons soy sauce

2 teaspoons grated fresh ginger

1 teaspoon minced garlic

1 teaspoon rice vinegar

½ teaspoon sugar

½ teaspoon sesame oil

1 cup corn kernels

¼ cup minced cilantro

50 round or square wonton wrappers

Soup:

4 cups corn broth (Corn and Clam Chowder, 48)

¼-inch-thick slices of fresh ginger

2 garlic cloves, peeled and slice thinly

1 tablespoon minced lemongrass

2 teaspoons raw sugar

1 teaspoon Thai fish sauce

1 large carrot, shredded

1 each medium summer squash and zucchini, seeds removed and julienned

1 serrano chili sliced very thinly

4 lime wedges

To make wontons, combine lobster, soy sauce, ginger, garlic, rice vinegar, sugar, and sesame oil in the bowl of a food processor; pulse until roughly chopped and combined. Fold corn and cilantro into the mixture.

Working with one wrapper at a time (cover remaining wrappers to keep them from drying), moisten outside edge of wrapper with water. Spoon 1½ teaspoons lobster mixture into center of wrapper. Fold wrapper over filling, corner to corner, making a triangle; pinch edges together to seal. Repeat procedure with remaining wrappers and lobster mixture (cover formed dumplings to keep them from drying).

Use 20 wontons to make soup. Freeze the remaining 30.

Combine broth, ginger, garlic, lemongrass, sugar, and fish sauce in a medium pot over medium heat. Bring to a simmer, stirring to dissolve the sugar. Reduce heat to low and steep broth for 15 minutes. Strain aromatics from broth. Compost aromatics. Bring broth back to a full boil over high heat. Add wontons and cook until they float back to the surface (3-4 minutes).

Divided julienned vegetables between four warm bowls. Divide cooked wontons and broth among bowls. Sprinkle each with cut chilis and serve soup hot with lime wedges.

Smoky roasted green beans and shallots

Since frozen green beans rarely (never?) taste as good as fresh if simply thawed and warmed in butter, I've taken to roasting them to give them a boost in both texture and flavor. The simple smoked paprika and honey vinaigrette adds color and contrast to the roasted beans. I typically serve these with roast chicken, but a vegetarian option would easily appear on the table if you stirred a cup of warm white beans in with the green ones and the vinaigrette.

Serves 4

1 pound frozen whole green beans

3 shallots, sliced into rings about ⅓-inch thick

⅓ cup olive oil

Kosher salt and freshly ground black pepper

2 tablespoons red wine or sherry vinegar

1 tablespoon honey

1½ teaspoons smoked paprika (sweet or hot)

1 teaspoon Dijon mustard

1 garlic clove, finely minced

¼ cup chopped toasted almonds (optional)

2 tablespoons roughly chopped fresh mint or parsley

Preheat oven to 450°. Set rack in center of oven. Line a heavy-bottomed, rimmed baking sheet with a silicone mat.

Place the beans and shallots on prepared baking sheet; drizzle with 2 tablespoons olive oil and season with salt and pepper; toss to combine. Transfer to oven and roast, tossing once or twice during cooking, until beans are tender and browned in spots and shallots are lightly caramelized (20 to 25 minutes). Transfer cooked vegetables to a serving bowl.

Use a blender to combine ¼ cup olive oil, vinegar, honey, paprika, mustard, and garlic. Drizzle vinaigrette over vegetables and toss to combine. Season with salt. Garnish with almonds and mint. Serve warm or at room temperature.

Meatless mains

Christine

Consider eating the whole plant when it's possible

Using up secondary edibles is not a new culinary skill. Most of our great-grandparents ate the greens as well as the beets, the chard stems as well as the leaves, and the carrot tops as well as their orange roots.

But as cooks began to get their vegetables from grocery stores more than their gardens, root-to-leaf cooking skills got lost. But since topped carrots (Carrot Top Salsa Verde, 178), leafy celery bunches (Date Night Fennel and Celery Salad, 44), and whole beet plants (Roasted Beet Reuben, 67) are regularly gracing the produce aisle and farmers markets, it's time for a refresher course.

You can learn a lot about root-to-leaf eating from zucchini.

The first thing to know is which part you don't want to eat. In zucchini's case that's the roots. They are knobby, hairy, and only appetizing to grubs. But zucchini's vines, leaves, flowers, fruits, and seeds are edible, in most cases, deliciously so.

Thriving zucchini plants have at least three male blossoms for every female bloom. When the pollinators have completed their rounds, fertilized female flowers fade as they bear fruit. Then there's not much left for the males to do. Well, except to be eaten, that is. They taste faintly of zucchini, only sweeter, and are rich and velvety.

How do you tell the male blossoms from the female? First, check the stem. Male blossoms have a long, slender stem; the female stem is shorter. Second, look at the point where the petals attach to the stem. Male blossoms have only a slender stalk, while female blossoms sport a small, bulbous area that houses the ovaries. Lastly, male blossoms have a stamen in the center of the flower.

Zucchini flowers are best picked in the morning the day they will be eaten. They tend to be closed in the early hours of the day, so there's less chance of bugs hiding inside. Do not wash them (water makes them wither), keep them refrigerated, and take care not to crush them. Just before cooking, remove the bitter stamens. I use a pair of kitchen tweezers, but if you have small fingers, reach inside and pinch them off. Give the blossoms a good shake for bugs and brush the outside with a dry paper towel.

Young squash leaves, young shoots, and their attached curly tendrils are also secondary edibles. Most often they are sautéed in oil, aromatics, and a bit of liquid. In Italy, that combination would be olive oil, garlic, and tomatoes. For a more Asian flare, you might add ginger, chilies, and coconut cream.

My favorite way to cook the zucchini itself is not to cook it at all. I shave the skin and flesh off with a julienne peeler to make Zucchini Pasta with Grated Tomato Sauce (66) and to make "noodles" for Lobster and Corn Wontons with Shredded Vegetables and Spicy Corn Broth (57). Both of those dishes leave me with just the seeds, which I simply blanch, spice, and roast (Roasted and Spiced Zucchini Seeds, 184) to use as either a garnish for soup or salad or the cook's reward for not wasting a single bit of zucchini.

Secondary edibles

Secondary edibles are the parts of ordinary fruits and vegetables that you can eat. They include: broccoli stems, carrot tops, cauliflower leaves, unfurled corn tassels, lima bean pods, onion leaves, parsley roots, sweet potato shoots, and watermelon rind.

Zucchini pasta with grated tomato sauce, page 66

Fried zucchini blossoms with fresh mozzarella and (optional) anchovies

Zucchini blossoms are a delicacy as well as a secondary edible. In the Mediterranean, they are stuffed with fresh mozzarella and salty (sustainable) anchovies and fried as I've done here. You can also chop them into frittatas and cut them into bright yellow-orange ribbons for salads.

Serves 4

20 zucchini blossoms

10 bite-sized fresh mozzarella balls (called bocconcini)

5 anchovy fillets (optional)

1½ cups neutral oil, such as canola or grapeseed

½ cup olive oil

½ cup all-purpose or white rice flour

¼ cup cornstarch

½ teaspoon baking powder

½ teaspoon kosher salt

¼ teaspoon freshly ground black pepper

¾ to 1 cup ice-cold sparkling water

Coarse sea salt

Prep the zucchini blossoms by removing the stamen from the center of each flower. Slice each mozzarella ball in half. Quarter each anchovy fillet. Stuff one piece of cheese and one piece of anchovy into the center of each blossom. Gently pull the leaves forward and give the ends a slight twist to keep the stuffing inside the flower while it's being fried. Repeat until all blossoms are stuffed.

Pour oils into a 3-quart pan. The oil should come up no higher than a third of the pan. Place pan over medium-high heat. Use a candy thermometer to gauge when the oil reaches 375°.

Set a baking rack lined with a recycled paper bag on the counter next to the stove.

In a medium bowl, whisk flour, cornstarch, baking powder, salt, and pepper. Slowly whisk in sparkling water until the mixture is the consistency of heavy cream.

When the oil is hot, dip one stuffed blossom into the batter, and immediately lower it into the hot oil. Repeat the process with 2 or 3 more flowers, taking care not to crowd them in the pan. Fry the blossoms in small batches until they are puffed, crisp, and golden (2-3 minutes). Use a slotted spoon to transfer them to the rack. Sprinkle the fried blossoms with coarse sea salt as soon as they come out of the oil. Serve immediately.

Thermometer substitute

If you don't have a candy thermometer, you can dip a tip of a wooden spoon in hot oil to see if it is ready for frying. If the oil bubbles around the spoon, it's ready.

Zucchini pasta with grated tomato sauce

On a hot day in the height of summer, zucchini steps in for pasta and a grated tomato sauce means I don't have to turn on the stove. Use Plan-over sauce either spooned on toast for a savory breakfast or with corn chips for a snack.

Serves 4
+ Plan-over 1 cup of sauce

3 pounds zucchini or summer squash

¼ cup kosher salt

4 pounds ripe tomatoes, halved

4 garlic cloves, peeled

1 cup tomato puree

4-6 tablespoons olive oil

Salt and pepper

Freshly grated Parmigiano-Reggiano cheese

6 basil leaves, torn into pieces

Use a mandolin or julienne peeler to slice the flesh of the squash into long strands. Combine strands with salt in a colander. Let sit for 1 hour. Rinse and set aside.

Grate cut sides of tomatoes on the large holes of a boxed grater into a bowl. Compost skins. Repeat until there are 4 cups of tomato pulp. Grate garlic on the small holes of the box grater into tomatoes. Stir in puree and 4 tablespoons olive oil. Season with salt and pepper.

Toss zucchini strands with 3 cups of raw tomato sauce in a large bowl. Drizzle with olive oil and season with salt and pepper. Serve with grated cheese and torn basil leaves.

Store remainder of sauce in an air-tight container in the refrigerator for up to 5 days.

Roasted beet Reuben

A corned beef Reuben was my food of choice after a night on the town with my friends in my younger years. Those nights are fewer and farther between now. This Reuben recipe matches my changing eating habits and metabolism, and my growing concern for sustainably sourced foods. Use any extra beet greens in either the Savory Double Dutch Baby (68), Harvest Mason Jar Salad with Greens and Grains (73), or One-pan Salmon with Spicy Creamed Greens and Tomatoes (130).

Makes 2 sandwiches
+ Plan-over beets for salad

Kosher salt

1 tablespoon slightly crushed coriander seeds

6 small red beets (1½ pounds total), scrubbed and trimmed, beet greens reserved

4 small yellow beets (1 pound total), scrubbed and trimmed, beet greens reserved

½ cup sauerkraut

2 tablespoons mayonnaise

2 teaspoons ketchup

1½ teaspoons sweet pickle relish

1 teaspoon fresh lemon juice

4 thin slices of hearty bread

1 tablespoon butter, softened

2 ounces shredded local Alpine-style cheese

Preheat the oven to 425°.

In a large baking dish, combine 2 cups of salt with coriander seeds. Nestle beets into mixture. Bake until beets are tender and their skins have loosened (45 to 50 minutes). Cool and peel beets. Slice 2 of the red roasted beets thinly.

Store Plan-over beets in an airtight container in the refrigerator for up to three days.

Shred ½ cup of the reserved beet greens and combine with sauerkraut in a bowl. Set aside.

Combine mayonnaise, ketchup, relish, and lemon juice in a small bowl. Set aside.

Place a large skillet over medium-high heat. Slather butter equally over one side of each piece of bread and place buttered sides down in the pan. On two of the slices spread half of the grated cheese and half of the sliced beets. On the other two slices, slather half of the mayonnaise mixture and pile on half of the sauerkraut.

Cook until the undersides of the bread are golden. Assemble the sandwiches by folding the halves onto each other. Slice each reuben on the diagonal. Serve warm.

Savory double Dutch baby

A Dutch baby is a cross between a pancake and a popover. It's baked in a hot pan until its filling rises well above the pan's edges and then rushed to the table for eaters to admire before it falls. Typically, it's slightly sweet and gets even sweeter with a dusting of powdered sugar or a drizzle of maple syrup. But it's just as good on the savory side. Chop herbs finely to get the best rise out of your baby.

Serves 4

8 eggs

3/4 cup milk

1/2 teaspoon kosher salt

1/2 teaspoon ground black pepper

1 cup plus 2 tablespoons all-purpose flour

1/4 cup finely grated tangy cheese (such as Pecorino or sharp cheddar)

1/4 cup finely minced herbs (parsley, thyme, basil, chives, and/or scallion tops or carrot tops)

3 tablespoons unsalted butter or rendered bacon fat

4 cups torn greens (beet, spinach, chard, kale, radish, mustard)

Olive oil

1 cup chopped tomato

Flaky sea salt

Chili pepper flakes

Place a 12-inch cast iron pan on the middle rack in the oven. Preheat oven to 425°.

Combine eggs, milk, salt, and pepper in a large bowl and whisk into a slight froth. Add flour and whisk until incorporated, scraping down the sides of the bowl as necessary. Whisk in cheese and herbs. Set aside.

Pull the hot pan out of the oven and drop butter or bacon grease into it. Swirl the pan so the fat coats its bottom. Slowly pour in batter and return the pan to the oven. Bake until the Dutch baby is puffed and golden (20 to 25 minutes).

Meanwhile, place greens on a baking tray and drizzle with oil. Use your hands to rub the oil into the greens. Roast the greens on a rack under the Dutch baby until they soften (8 to 10 minutes). Remove greens from the oven, toss with tomatoes, sea salt, and chili pepper flakes to taste.

When the Dutch baby is cooked, fill its center with the greens mixture and serve immediately.

den and ruby beets
h goat cheese, pistachios
l microgreens,
ge 70

Golden and ruby beets with goat cheese, pistachios, and microgreens

Serves 4-6

4 small cooked red beets

4 small cooked golden beets

Honey Orange Blossom Dressing (174)

1½ cups microgreens

3 ounces fresh local goat cheese, crumbled

¼ cup shelled pistachios

This is my go-to communal picnic contribution because it's made with mostly local ingredients, it travels well, and it's really beautiful on a buffet table.

Slice beets in ¼-inch-thick slices and arrange in concentric circles on a serving platter. When ready to serve, shake vinaigrette and pour ⅔ of it over the beets. Top with microgreens, goat cheese, and pistachios. Drizzle the remaining vinaigrette over salad and serve.

Swiss chard stem, thyme, and Parmesan cheese spread tartines

When I found my first bunch of rainbow chard, I was such a non-gardener that I thanked the farmer for giving me a couple leaves each with red, pink, yellow, and white stems. She giggled and explained they grow that way. I make these open-faced sandwiches the day after I make Rainbow Chard-Wrapped Flaky White Fish with Lemon, Parsley, and Hazelnut Relish (111) or Harvest Mason Jar Salad with Grains and Greens (73). Don't rush, the stems are richer and more supple if cooked the full hour in oil.

Makes 2 tartines
+ Plan-over 1 cup of cheese spread

2½ cups very finely grated Parmesan cheese

½ cup extra virgin olive oil

¼ cup dry white wine

12 naked Swiss chard stems

1 teaspoon fresh thyme leaves

Sea salt

Black pepper

2 1-inch-thick slices of toastable bread

Combine cheese, 3 tablespoons olive oil, and wine in a bowl. Mix well. Set aside.

Slice the chard stems thinly and transfer to a sauté pan with ¼ cup of olive oil. Place pan over medium heat until oil warms and stems start to sizzle. Immediately drop the heat to low and cook stems slowly until soft (60 to 90 minutes). Once the stems soften, add ½ teaspoon thyme leaves to pan. Cook another 15 minutes. Remove from heat.

Toast the bread and slather ¼ cup of cheese spread on each piece. Spread half of the cooked chard stems on each tartine and garnish with remaining thyme leaves. Serve warm.

Store the extra cheese spread in a glass jar in the refrigerator for up to two weeks. Use as a white pizza topping.

Christine

Understand what a sell-by date really means

The "sell by," "best before," and "use by" dates stamped on commercial food packaging don't actually mean what nine out of ten Americans think they do.

Popularized in the 1970s, these date stamps were not intended to be an indication of a food's microbial safety. They were designed to be an indication of when the packaged food would be at its peak flavor, not when it poses a mortal threat to an eater.

"Sell by" dates aren't meant for consumer use at all. They are tools to help retailers ensure proper product turnover when stocking shelves. "Best by" dates are set by the manufacturer as suggestions for when to consume the food by for best flavor or quality. A "use by" date is the last date recommended for the product to be at its peak quality as determined by the manufacturer.

There is no standard practice for how manufacturers set these dates—some are determined in labs by scientists, others in conference rooms by taste testers. Given that Americans are likely to chuck food past the sell-by date just to buy more of the same, the food industry has little financial incentive to clarify the situation.

A study published by Harvard University in 2016 found that over one third of the US population (37 percent) usually throws away food because it is close to or past the date on the package. Over twice that number report occasionally discarding food based on date labels with younger consumers (age 18-34) being more likely than older consumers to throw away food based on the date label.

The Natural Resources Defense Council argues these imprints do more harm than good to the American food system. They add significantly to the 160 billion pounds of food wasted annually, hinder food recovery and redistribution efforts, and squander energy required to produce, transport, and store food across the country. The organization is working to establish a reliable, coherent dating system that puts both freshness and food safety dates (where necessary) in predictable spots on all packaging.

But that will take congressional action, so what's an eater to do in the meantime? First and foremost, shop in moderation. "Resist that great buy if it means you are picking up an item in a quantity that you can't reasonably consume," said JoAnne Berkenkamp, senior advocate in the Natural Resources Defense Council's Food and Agriculture Program, adding that sticking to a list is another good way to avoid overbuying.

And if you do buy in bulk, have a detailed plan for using up every last bite. If, for example, you buy the huge container of baby spinach for a salad on Monday, plan to make Creamy Potato and Spinach Curry (75) for Thursday.

Instead of tossing food because of a date stamp, "Trust your senses more," says Berkenkamp. Is the food discolored? Does it smell off?

And finally, it pays to understand the intricacies of your refrigerator. Things that will rot should go in the low humidity drawer, and things that will wilt should be placed in the high humidity drawer. For efficiency's sake, neither drawer should ever be more than two-thirds full. Pack your refrigerator and your freezer responsibly, and you'll both save money and keep wholesome food out of the landfill.

Whole spices

To stretch the life of expensive spices, buy them whole, and store them in a dry, dark place. Roasting them in a dry pan and grinding them just before use gives you the biggest flavor for your buck every time.

Harvest mason jar salad with grains and greens

You'll need roasted squash, pre-cooked grains, and 4 wide-mouthed mason jars with lids for this recipe. To prevent the dressing from soaking your greens, put it in the bottom of the jars, followed by harder, non-absorbent vegetables or fruits that need a little acid to keep from oxidizing. Layer cooked whole grains, legumes, cheese, nuts, and berries. Finish the packing job with greens just before you tighten the lid. This salad will keep in the refrigerator for 2 to 3 days.

Makes 4 salads

+ Plan-over chard stems for Swiss Chard Stem, Thyme, and Parmesan Cheese Spread Tartines, 71

Vinaigrette:

- 3 tablespoons balsamic vinegar
- 1 tablespoon maple syrup
- 1 tablespoon minced shallot
- 1 teaspoon Dijon mustard
- ½ teaspoon kosher salt
- ¼ teaspoon ground black pepper
- ¼ cup canola oil
- ¼ cup olive oil

Salad:

- 1 fennel bulb, sliced thinly
- 1 tart apple, sliced thinly
- 2 cups roasted vegetables (butternut squash, beets, parsnip, corn, squash, sweet potato)
- 1 cup roasted, salted pumpkin seeds
- 4 ounces crumbled goat cheese
- ½ cup dried cranberries
- 2 cups cooked barley, farro, or wheat berries
- 8 cups chopped Lacitino kale, rainbow Swiss chard, or spinach

To make the dressing, whisk vinegar, maple syrup, shallot, mustard, salt, and pepper. Combine oils in a measuring cup and whisk into vinegar mixture until it has emulsified and is slightly thickened. Divide vinaigrette equally among jars.

Toss the fennel and apples in the bowl you used to make vinaigrette. Divide among jars. Layer ½ cup of roasted vegetables in each jar followed by ¼ cup pumpkin seeds, 1 ounce goat cheese, 2 tablespoons cranberries, and ½ cup cooked whole grains. Pack 2 cups greens leaving 2 to 3 inches of headroom in each jar. Cover and refrigerate until ready to use.

To eat, give the jar a really good shake, pour contents out onto a plate, and dig in.

Creamy potato and spinach curry

This recipe uses up three items I tend to buy too much of when grocery shopping: baby spinach, new potatoes, and yogurt.

Serves 6

½ pound baby leaf spinach

1 pound small new potatoes, quartered

Kosher salt and black pepper

2 tablespoons neutral oil

1 large onion, finely chopped

2 large garlic cloves, finely chopped

1 teaspoon black mustard seeds

1 teaspoon ground coriander

1 teaspoon garam masala

½ to 1 teaspoon red chili flakes, to taste

½ teaspoon ground turmeric

½ teaspoon ground cumin

2 tablespoons butter

1 cup whole or reduced fat Greek yogurt

1-inch piece of fresh ginger, peeled and grated

Fresh mint leaves, ½ red chili, sliced, and lemon or lime wedges for garnish

Put spinach in a colander positioned in the sink.

Place potatoes in medium pot with salted cold water. Bring pot to a boil, cook until potatoes are just tender (8 to 10 minutes). Drain potatoes over colander of spinach to wilt the leaves.

Remove potatoes from the colander and prick potatoes with a fork to roughen the skins so the curry sauce will stick to them. Set aside.

Refresh spinach leaves with cold water and squeeze to remove excess water. Roughly chop and set aside.

Heat oil in a large sauté pan over medium heat. Sauté onion and a pinch of salt and until golden (6 to 8 minutes). Add garlic and spices, stirring for 1 minute. Add butter and potatoes, stir to coat. Cook for 10 minutes, stirring occasionally so spices don't burn. Turn heat to its lowest setting.

Combine yogurt, ginger, and salt and pepper to taste. Stir mixture into pan with 2 tablespoons of water and heat gently (to prevent the yogurt from curdling) until potatoes are tender and sauce has thickened (5 minutes). Stir reserved wilted spinach into curry. Scatter mint and sliced chili over top. Serve warm with lemon or lime wedges.

Masoor moong dal

While this recipe given to me by chef Raj Mandekar of Tulsi, a great Indian Restaurant in Kittery, requires quite a few ingredients, buying spices, beans, and lentils in small quantities from the bulk bins cuts down on unnecessary packaging.

Serves 4

½ cup moong dal (dried, skinned, split yellow mung beans)

½ cup masoor dal (dried, split red lentils)

1½ tablespoons vegetable oil

2 teaspoons whole cumin seeds

4 whole, dried chili peppers (lal mirch, small reddish brown chilis)

4 cloves garlic, crushed

½ teaspoon asafetida powder

½ cup thinly sliced yellow onion

1 teaspoon turmeric

2 tablespoons chopped jalapeño chiles (optional)

10 fresh curry leaves

4 dried bay leaves

½ cup chopped fresh tomatoes

1 teaspoon kosher salt

½ teaspoon freshly toasted and finely ground cumin powder

½ cup chopped cilantro leaves

4 Any Occasion Flatbread (18)

Bring 5 cups of water to a boil in a large saucepan over high heat. Add moong and masoor dal. Cook for 10 minutes, skimming any foam from the top. Set aside.

Place a medium skillet over medium-high heat and add the oil. When the oil is hot, add cumin seeds and dried chili peppers and let them sizzle briefly (5 to 7 seconds); the chilies will turn black. Immediately add the garlic and cook until lightly brown (30 seconds). Add the asafetida and onions. Cook the onions until they are golden brown (3 to 4 minutes).

Remove the pan from the heat, add the turmeric, jalapeño chiles (if using), curry and bay leaves. Return the pan to medium-high heat, and cook for 2 minutes. Add the tomatoes and cook them until they soften but do not completely lose their shape (2 minutes).

Add the onion, tomato and spice mixture to the dal pot. Stir in the salt. Bring to a simmer and cook until the dal are softened (10 to 12 minutes). If you like them quite soft, you may need to add more water and let them cook longer.

To prepare the cumin powder, place the whole seeds in a dry skillet over medium-high heat. As soon as you smell the cumin, remove the skillet from the burner. Pour the seeds into a spice grinder (I use a small Krups coffee grinder) or a mortar and pestle and grind them to a fine powder.

Just before serving, stir in the freshly toasted cumin powder. Garnish the dal with chopped cilantro leaves and serve hot with warm flatbread.

Smoky baked mac and cheese

My kids have always preferred homemade mac and cheese to the boxed variety. This recipe has evolved to be more flavorful over the years as we've mixed and matched cheeses we've come to love along the way. The extra cheese sauce in this recipe, reheated, dolls up weeknight broccoli or cauliflower in two minutes flat.

Serves 4 to 6
+ Plan-over 1 cup cheese sauce

1 pound shaped pasta

¼ cup (½ stick) butter plus more for buttering dish

⅓ cup flour

1 tablespoon powdered mustard (1 tablespoon plus 1 teaspoon of prepared mustard)

5 cups milk (whole is best but 2% is okay)

1 teaspoon Worcestershire sauce

5 ounces smoked cheddar cheese, grated

5 ounces yellow mild cheddar cheese, grated

5 ounces Alpine cheese, grated

5 ounces stretchy cheese like Monterey Jack, grated

½ to 1 teaspoon kosher salt

¼ teaspoon white pepper

⅛ teaspoon cayenne pepper

Preheat the oven to 350°. Butter the bottom and sides of a 9-by-13-inch casserole dish.

Bring a large pot of salted water to a boil and cook the pasta to al dente, 9 to 12 minutes, depending on the pasta type. Drain.

While the pasta is cooking, in a separate pot, melt the butter. Whisk in the flour and mustard and keep whisking for about 5 minutes to cook out the floury taste. Whisk in the milk and Worcestershire sauce. Simmer for 10 minutes.

Combine all of the cheeses. Slowly add ¾ of the cheese to the sauce, a handful at a time, stirring after each addition. Season with salt and peppers. Remove one cup of cheese sauce for Plan-over purposes. Cool and refrigerate for up to 3 days.

Fold the pasta into the remainder of the hot cheese sauce and pour into prepared casserole dish. Top with remaining cheese.

Bake the macaroni and cheese for 30 minutes until the cheese on the top has browned a bit and the sauce is bubbling up around the edges. Remove from oven and cool for 5 minutes before serving.

Spanish potato tortilla

This potato omelet is widely available at almost any time in Spain. I like it best for dinner served with a spicy condiment (Corn Cilantro Pesto, 177 or Carrot Top Salsa Verde, 178) and a lightly dressed salad. The yolks of fresh eggs from pasture chickens combine with the yellow flesh of the Yukon Gold potatoes, which work best for this dish because of their lower starch content, to give the finished product a sunny glow.

Serves 4-6

¾ cup olive oil

7 or 8 medium Yukon Gold potatoes, peeled and sliced uniformly to a ⅛-inch thickness

1 medium sized sweet onion, peeled, halved and sliced uniformly to a ⅛-inch thickness

6 large, fresh, pastured eggs

1½ teaspoon kosher salt

½ teaspoon fresh ground pepper

Preheat oven to 350°.

Place olive oil in a oven-safe 12-inch frying pan over medium-high heat. When the oil is hot but not smoking, drop one potato slice into it. If it sizzles rapidly it is ready to use. Working in batches, put about 1½ cups of sliced potatoes into the hot oil. Cook them for 2 to 3 minutes until they are somewhat soft, but not at all crispy. Remove the potatoes from the hot oil with a slotted spoon and place them in a large bowl. Repeat until all of the potatoes have been par-cooked in the oil. Set them aside to cool slightly.

Remove all but 2 tablespoons of the olive oil from the frying pan and sauté the onions until they are soft and slightly caramelized (4 to 6 minutes).

While the onions are cooking, beat 6 eggs until they are well combined. Add salt and pepper. Add the egg mixture to the par-cooked potatoes. Using a rubber spatula, fully coat the potatoes with the egg mixture, being very careful to keep the potatoes slices intact.

Turn the heat under the pan of sautéing onions to medium-high. Add the egg and potato mixture to the pan, taking care to spread it evenly. In a couple of places towards the middle of the pan, use a spatula to move some of the potatoes around so that more of the egg mixture hits the heat. This will insure the eggs are fully cooked in the end.

Once the bottom of the tortilla has set and has achieved a nice golden brown color. Place the pan into the oven and cook until the eggs have set completely (10 to 12 minutes).

Remove the tortilla from the oven and transfer it to a clean serving platter. You can serve this dish hot, at room temperature or cold. But it is best to let it sit for 3-4 minutes before slicing it like a pie.

Christine

The joy of cooking with what's left in the bottle

My husband and I were married on New Year's Eve 1994. We picked that particular night because it provides an airtight excuse for us to enjoy quiet at-home New Year's celebrations instead of being pressured into braving drunken crowds and risking dangerous roads.

Over the years, romantic candlelight dinners have morphed into raucous family game nights with our teens in front of the fire, but popping the bubbly at midnight has been a constant. Twenty years ago, the two of us could easily polish off the bottle (maybe even two), but lately there's been significant leftovers that go flat as we've not found a good wine gadget that keeps the bubbles in the bottle. I am too old to pretend I like the cheap stuff, so wasted champagne means wasted money if I don't find a good use for it. So I do.

A quick way is to fake effervescence by mixing it with sparkling citrus soda and a splash of orange juice for New Year's Day brunch mimosas. Seriously, no one will know.

But the easiest way to repurpose a bottle of flat champagne is pour it into a clean, wide-mouthed mason jar, cover it with few layers of cheese cloth, place it in a cool, dark place, and let it make its own way to vinegar in a few weeks' time. I start tasting it after three weeks to see if it's turned. When it has, I transfer the vinegar to a bottle with a stopper for safekeeping in the pantry for up to six months. I've learned the hard way that Champagne vinegar generally has higher acidity (7 percent) than either white or apple cider vinegar (5 percent), so a little goes a long way when using it in a vinaigrette.

Bubbly is, by definition, white wine at its core and can therefore be used as such (Peas Three Ways Risotto, 81). If you've got a full cup, pour it in a pot with some minced shallot, two pounds of mussels and a sprinkling of fresh parsley, a combination that would give you dinner in 15 minutes flat. You can tart up that simple dish up with smoked paprika, cream and tomatoes (Smoky Mussels with Thyme and Tomatoes, 126) to almost effortlessly impress guests. Ask them to bring the wine.

It's probably wise to avoid the actual dregs in any bottle of wine, but for the love of Bacchus, don't ever dump even the last bit of wine down the drain. Pour it into an ice cube tray and freeze it in a perfect portion to help you deglaze the pan after you've seared a piece of protein or when a sauce you've made needs a drop of something acidic.

Wine substitute

Out of red wine and your recipe calls for 1 cup? Substitute ¾ cup red grape juice mixed with 2 tablespoons each of red wine vinegar and water for marinades or 1 cup beef stock or beer for sauces and stews. For 1 cup of white wine, substitute ¾ cups apple juice mixed with ¼ cup lemon juice or white wine vinegar for marinades; or 1 cup chicken, vegetable, or fish stock for sauces and stews.

Peas three ways risotto

Get your peas straight, man. Shell the garden-variety English ones. Remove the strings from sugar snap peas. And, as explained by their French name, mange tout *(eat all), snow peas can be eaten in their entirety. This recipe uses only English peas, but does so three ways (peas, broth, and puree) in an homage to their short-lived but oh so flavorful season.*

Serves 4 to 6

1 pound English peas in their pods

3 tablespoons unsalted butter

2 tablespoons olive oil

¼ cup minced shallot

1 cup short-grain rice (such as Arborio)

½ cup dry white wine

½ cup grated hard Italian cheese (Pecorino or Parmesan)

Zest of 1 lemon and 1 tablespoon lemon juice

Kosher salt and black pepper

2 tablespoons chopped mint

Shell peas and set peas and shells aside.

Place a large pot filled with 4 cups of water and 1 tablespoon kosher salt over high heat. When water comes to a rolling boil, add half of the empty pods (but no strings or stems). Blanch for 60 seconds. Remove pods from water with a slotted spoon and shock them in ice water.

Transfer shocked pods to a blender and puree with ½ cup of blanching water. Strain through a fine mesh sieve, compost solids, and set bright green puree aside.

Add remaining empty pods as well as all strings and stems into the large pot of blanching water. Place it over high heat. Bring to a boil. Reduce heat to medium and simmer for 30 minutes. Cool slightly, and strain broth into a smaller saucepan. Compost solids and keep pea pod broth warm over low heat.

Once again, place the large pot over medium-high heat. Melt 1 tablespoon of butter in 2 tablespoons olive oil. When the butter begins to foam, stir in shallots, and cook until softened (2 to 3 minutes). Stir in rice. Cook until the rice absorbs the fat and turns translucent (1 minute). Add wine and cook until it evaporates (1 minute).

Begin adding the reserved warm pea pod broth, ½ cup at a time, stirring regularly and allowing the stock to be fully absorbed before adding more. Continue stirring until all stock has been added (15 to 18 minutes). Risotto will be creamy and grains of rice should be tender but not mushy.

Stir in reserved peas, ¼ cup cheese, lemon zest and juice, and remaining 2 tablespoons of butter. Cover pot and let risotto sit (2 to 3 minutes). The peas will cook in the residual heat.

Season with salt and pepper. Stir in mint. Garnish each dish with an artful drizzle of pea pod puree and a sprinkle of cheese, and serve immediately.

Cauliflower "polenta" with mushrooms

Cauliflower rice is a popular way to trick your palate into thinking you're eating carbs when you are trying to cut back on them. This is a similar tactic with an Italian taste profile.

Serves 4

1½ cups flat champagne or white wine

1½ ounces dried porcini or chanterelle mushrooms

1 large head cauliflower, trimmed and cut into small florets

4 tablespoons softened butter

2 tablespoons olive oil

1 pound crimini mushrooms, trimmed and sliced

Kosher salt and black pepper

1 large shallot, minced

2 tablespoons mascarpone or cream cheese

2 teaspoons finely chopped fresh thyme

1 cup grated Parmesan or Pecorino cheese

Heat champagne or wine in a medium saucepan over high heat until it boils. Use a glass measuring cup to remove ½ cup of hot wine. Add dried mushrooms to the measuring cup to soak and reconstitute for 20 minutes. Drain mushrooms (saving liquid) and chop finely.

Add cauliflower to saucepan with remainder of hot wine, bring to a boil over high heat. Cook, stirring occasionally, until cauliflower is tender (8 to 10 minutes).

In a sauté pan, melt 1 tablespoon of butter in 2 tablespoons of olive oil over medium-high heat until it foams. Add crimini mushrooms, sprinkle with salt and pepper. Cook, stirring occasionally until mushrooms are tender and slightly browned (6 to 8 minutes). Add shallots and reconstituted mushrooms. Cook, stirring, for 1 minute. Add reserved mushroom champagne mixture and simmer until half of the liquid has evaporated. Keep warm.

Transfer the cooked cauliflower to the bowl of a food processor in batches. Add ¼ cup cooking liquid and pulse each batch until cauliflower puree is the consistency of polenta. Scrape each batch into a large, warm bowl. Add remaining 3 tablespoons of softened butter, mascarpone or cream cheese, thyme and ¾ cup grated cheese and stir.

Spoon "polenta" into warm bowls, top with mushrooms and remaining grated cheese, and serve.

Bulgogi burgers with quick pickles and spicy mayonnaise, page 97

Meat

Christine

Cutting meat portions is better for you and the planet

I feed a family of committed omnivores, but I can't ignore the growing evidence pointing to the benefits, for our bodies and the planet, of eating less meat.

The American Cancer Society and the American Heart and Diabetes Associations profess the medical merits of eating less red meat (even less than the 3-ounce, twice-weekly USDA Dietary Guidelines). The U.N. Food and Agriculture Organization argues that 14.5 percent of all global greenhouse gas pollution can be attributed to conventional production of livestock for food.

Full-on vegetarianism—while arguably one of the most climate-impactful steps an eater can take—is not on the menu for us near term. That line drawn, I've developed a rotation of culinary tricks to keep my family's animal protein consumption in check. This mindset is called *reducetarianism*.

I don't talk about Meatless Mondays because that just draws attention to what's absent from the table, but a meal made up of ravioli, gnocchi or tortellini with a chunky marinara sauce, a big salad, and garlic bread on the side sate the masses nonetheless.

Mustardy Pork Schnitzel (88) is a cunning way to disguise small portions of pork as plate-filling pieces of meat. I cut 16 ounces of pork loin into five slices, pound each piece thin, dip them in flour, buttermilk, and breadcrumbs, and quickly pan-fry each. Boiled and buttered local potatoes and a vinegary, crunchy cabbage slaw round out that meal.

I employ well-spiced ethnic culinary traditions that use meat as more of a condiment than as an anchor. Think Marinated Pork Cuban Subs (89), Asian stir-fries dotted with pieces of seafood, or Indian curries, where chunks of lamb share the sauce with potatoes, legumes, and vegetables.

I use smoky cured pork products in moderation to ramp up the flavors of pasta in a variety of ways (Pasta Carbonara-ish, 94) and give distinction to left-over concoctions (Bacon Bubble and Squeak Cakes, 92).

When I do serve beef, it's typically burgers (Bulgogi burger recipe, 97) or a slow-roasted lesser cut that gets spread over a couple of meals (Fast Beef Bourguignon, 90 or Shredded Beef, Sweet Potato, and Black Bean Empanadas, 91). I do make steak on occasion, but they're never much bigger than 1¼ pounds for the four of us. The threefold sleight of hand here is to season it very well with kosher salt and black pepper long before cooking it, to let it rest for at least five minutes after it's done cooking, and finally, to cut it as thin on the bias as possible. The seasoning gives it a beefier flavor, the resting makes the meat juicier in appearance, and an ample number of slices help trick my carnivorous family into thinking there's more meat on the plate than there really is. All these little steps help us all reach my reducetarian goals.

Modern Meat Vocabulary

Cage-free means the chicken was not raised in a cage, but doesn't necessarily mean they have access to the outdoors.
Certified humane means the farmer has proven she cares for her livestock in line with standards set by American Humane Association.
Certified organic means the animal was not injected with hormones and its feed did not contain animal by-products, antibiotics, or genetically engineered grains and was not grown using persistent pesticides or chemical fertilizers.
Free-range means the chicken has some access to the outside.
Grass-fed means the cow has eaten grass or hay for the majority of its life.
Natural, as defined by the USDA, means the meat contains no artificial ingredient or added color and is only minimally processed.
Pasture-raised means the animal roamed freely in its natural environment eating grasses and other plants that their bodies are adapted to digest.
Reducetarian describes a carnivore attempting to cut back on the amount of animal protein he consumes.
USDA grades mean the conventionally raised beef is labeled as Prime, Choice, and Select based on the amount of marbling (the thin white streaks of fat found between the muscles that melt and baste the meat when heated) it contains. Prime, which has the most marbling and therefore the best taste and tenderness, is the most expensive.

Mustardy pork schnitzel

This recipe is adapted from one my friend Rob Martin, chef at When Pigs Fly Pizzeria in Kittery, gave me. He uses lean pork loin from locally raised pigs to make his very popular schnitzel dishes. You can easily swap boneless, skinless chicken thighs for the pork.

Serves 4

5 (3-ounce) slices of pork loin

Kosher salt and freshly ground black pepper

1 cup white-whole wheat flour

1 cup buttermilk

2 tablespoons coarse mustard

2 teaspoons baking soda

2 cups plain bread crumbs

¼ cup olive oil for frying

Lemon wedges and chopped parsley for garnish (optional)

Use a meat mallet to pound loins to ¼-inch thickness. Season with salt and pepper.

Pour flour into one flat bowl. Combine buttermilk, mustard, and baking soda in a second flat bowl. Combine crumbs, one teaspoon of salt, and ½ teaspoon pepper in a third flat bowl.

Dredge both sides of each flattened piece of pork first in flour, then in the buttermilk mixture, and finally in the breadcrumb mixture. Let breaded pork rest for 30 minutes.

Heat oil in a large skillet (a 14-inch skillet should accommodate all 4 pieces at once) over medium heat. Place breaded pork into the oil and fry until breading is just golden brown (3 to 4 minutes). Flip cutlets. Cook until second sides of the cutlets are golden, (3 to 4 minutes). Drain schnitzel on torn paper bags or paper towels.

Serve hot with lemon and parsley.

Marinated pork Cuban subs

These sandwiches are perfect for a reducetarian gathering as you can assemble them ahead of time and simply grill them as needed. They have tons of flavor and very little meat in the mix per person. I think half of one of these sandwiches is plenty, but my son disagrees.

Serves 4-8

1 cup loosely packed cilantro

¼ cup loosely packed mint leaves

8 garlic cloves, smashed

¼ cup loosely packed fresh oregano leaves

2 teaspoons ground cumin

½ cup olive oil

Zest and juice of 3 limes

Zest and juice of 1 orange

1 teaspoon kosher salt

½ teaspoon ground black pepper

1½ pounds bone-in pork shoulder

4 hoagie rolls

2 tablespoons yellow mustard

10 thin dill pickle slices, approximately 2 whole pickles

¼ pound provolone cheese, thinly sliced

Combine cilantro, mint, garlic, oregano, and cumin in the bowl of a food processor and pulse until all are finely chopped. Add this mixture to a bowl and stir in oil, citrus zest and juice, and salt and pepper. Add pork. Rub the marinade into all sides of the meat, cover and refrigerate overnight.

Preheat oven to 425°. Place a wire rack over a rimmed baking sheet. Transfer pork from marinade to wire rack and discard the marinade. Roast the pork for 30 minutes. Reduce heat to 375°. Roast until meat reaches an internal temperature of 145° (1 to 1 ¼ hours). Transfer pork to a cutting board, cover with aluminum foil, and let it rest 20 minutes. Cut pork close to the bone to free large pieces. Slice those pieces against the grain of the meat.

To assemble the sandwiches, slice rolls horizontally leaving one edge intact. Lay the bread open and slather the inside of each roll with mustard. Divide sliced pork, pickles and cheese among the rolls. Close sandwiches and cover until you are ready to grill them.

Place the sandwiches over a hot grill and place something heavy, like a brick wrapped in foil, on top to weigh each one down. Grill until cheese is melted and bread is toasted. Slice sandwiches diagonally and serve.

Meat thermometers

To get an accurate temperature on a roasting bone-in piece of meat, the thermometer must be pushed firmly into the thickest, meatiest part of the roast not near the bone. I use a meat thermometer that can handle the heat of the oven. It remains inserted into the meat throughout the roasting time and reports the rising temperature to a device outside the oven so that I am not wasting oven energy opening the door to take the roast's temperature.

Fast beef bourguignon

Beef bourguignon is typically a long, slow winter braise requiring 3 to 4 hours in the oven. Maine Chef Benjamin Hasty of Thistle Pig in Berwick speeds up the dish by using leftover braised meat, cutting the total time for his version to just an hour. He contends that buying bigger hunks of beef like 4- or 5-pound shoulder roasts or bottom rounds is a sustainable practice if coupled with longer-term dinner planning. He advises home cooks to season these cuts with a favorite brine, rub, or marinade, cook them once using a slow, low-heat method to draw out the flavor and tenderize the meat, then divide the meat to be served in several dishes over the course of the week. The meat can also be wrapped and frozen.

Serves 4

2 large carrots

2 medium potatoes

3 tablespoons canola oil

16 to 24 ounces cooked beef shoulder, cut into 1-inch cubes

Flour or cornstarch to dredge

4 strips of thinly sliced bacon, diced

1 cup button mushrooms, cut into quarters

1 garlic clove, smashed

2 tablespoons tomato paste

1 cup red wine

4 cups beef stock

1 cup frozen pearl onions

2 tablespoons softened butter

¼ teaspoon minced thyme leaves

Black pepper and kosher salt

Peel and slice carrots into ¼-inch discs. Peel and cut potatoes into ½-inch cubes. Place a steam basket in a medium-sized pot, add 1 inch of water to the pan. Layer carrots in the basket first and top with potatoes. Place the pot, covered, over medium-high heat. Steam vegetables until tender (12 to 15 minutes). Set aside.

As the vegetables cook, heat the oil in a large Dutch oven over high heat until smoking. Dredge cooked beef in flour or cornstarch. Add dredged beef, bacon, mushrooms, and garlic to hot oil. Cook until beef is browned, mushrooms are caramelized, and bacon has rendered its fat and has begun to crisp (5 to 7 minutes).

Stir in tomato paste and cook for 1 minute. Add wine and reduce heat to medium. Reduce wine by one quarter (3 to 4 minutes). Add stock, turn heat to medium-high, reduce liquid by half (12 to 15 minutes). Add onions, carrots, and potatoes, bring mixture back to a simmer, and cook until liquid coats the back of a spoon (15 to 20 minutes). Remove from heat.

Whisk pieces of butter into the sauce until it is thick and silky. Add fresh thyme. Adjust seasoning. Serve hot.

Shredded beef, sweet potato, and black bean empanadas

If I am making braised beef, this is what I plan to do with some of the leftovers. I skim the fat from the braising liquid and use it to add flavor and color to the pastry dough.

Makes 12 pastries

Dough:

- 2 1/4 cups unbleached all-purpose flour
- 1 1/2 teaspoons kosher salt
- 1/2 cup cold reserved beef fat from braise (you can substitute cold unsalted butter, cut into 1/2-inch pieces)
- 1 tablespoon distilled white vinegar
- 1/3 cup ice water
- 1 egg white, beaten with 1 tablespoon water
- Toasted cumin seeds, for garnish
- Flaky sea salt, for garnish

Filling:

- 1 cup small diced sweet potato, steamed until tender
- Kosher salt
- 1/2 cup shredded braised beef
- 1/2 cup cooked black beans
- 1/2 cup shredded smoked cheddar cheese
- 2 tablespoons minced chipotle chili in adobo sauce
- 2 tablespoons minced cilantro
- 1 teaspoon orange zest
- Lime wedges, Sour Cream, and Corn Cilantro Pesto (177) for serving

Mix the flour and salt in a food processor. Add fat and pulse. Add vinegar and pulse. Add water in increments, pulsing until a clumpy dough forms. Split the dough into two large balls, flatten slightly into disks. Let rest 30 minutes. While the dough rests, make the filling by combining all ingredients in a bowl.

To assemble, roll dough into a thin sheet and cut out 4-inch circles using a biscuit or cookie cutter. Place a scant 1/4 cup of filling in the middle of each. Brush egg white around the edge of each circle of dough, fold each circle in half over filling, and seal edges by pinching dough together with a fork.

Refrigerate empanadas for 30 minutes. Preheat oven to 375°. Place empanadas on a lined baking sheet. Coat with egg white and sprinkle with cumin seeds and flaky salt. Bake until golden brown (18 to 20 minutes). Serve hot with lime wedges, sour cream, and Corn and Cilantro Pesto (177).

Bacon bubble and squeak cakes

The proverbial English recipe for using up vegetables left over from a traditional Sunday roast, "bubble and squeak" got its name from the noises these ingredients make while frying. This version can vary based on what you've got in the fridge. In the version in the photograph, I tossed in pre-dressed kale, cabbage, Brussels sprout salad, maple-glazed carrots, and parsnips.

Serves 4

¼ cup chopped bacon

1 red onion, finely chopped

2 cups leftover mashed potatoes

2 cups leftover, mixed, cooked vegetables, chopped into small pieces (parsnips, green beans, Brussels sprouts, cabbage, carrots, cauliflower, broccoli, peas)

Kosher salt and black pepper

2 tablespoons chopped herbs (chives, parsley, thyme, basil, chervil)

½ cup grated hard cheese (Parmiggiano-Reggiano or aged cheddar)

2 tablespoons melted butter

½ cup all-purpose flour

Place bacon in a large skillet and cook over medium heat until it starts to crisp (4 to 5 minutes). Add onions and cook until they soften (4 to 5 minutes). Remove the pan from heat and transfer bacon and onions to a large bowl, leaving bacon grease in skillet.

Add the mashed potato and cooked vegetables to the bowl and season well with salt and pepper. Stir in herbs, cheese, and butter. Divide the mixture into 8 portions. Shape each one into a cake, roughly 1 inch thick.

Spread flour on a plate and coat each cake with it on both sides. Fry the cakes in the fat remaining in the skillet over medium-high heat until warmed through and golden (3 to 4 minutes per side). Sprinkle with salt. Serve warm.

Pasta carbonara-ish

A French video depicting the making of spaghetti alla carbonara—a popular Italian dish consisting of spaghetti, bacon, eggs, Pecorino cheese and freshly ground black pepper—raised Italian social media ire when the Frenchman boiled the pasta in the same pot as the bacon and finished the dish with crème fraîche. While my recipe follows the Roman way of folding hot pasta into raw eggs to make a luscious sauce, I use whichever pasta, cured meat, and hard cheese I happen to have on hand to avoid wasting the time, money, and energy required to run to the store for specific ingredients.

Serves 4

2 tablespoons olive oil

½ cup cubed pancetta, smoky and/or cured bacon, guanciale, chorizo, chourico, or kielbasa

Kosher salt

1 pound dried pasta

4 whole eggs and 1 egg yolk

½ cup plus 2 tablespoons grated hard cheese (such as Pecorino, Parmesan, Grana Padano, dry Jack, Asiago, Manchego, aged Gouda, or any local grating cheeses)

Freshly ground black pepper

Nutmeg

Heat oil in a large skillet over medium heat, add cured meat, and cook until golden (4 to 5 minutes). Remove pan from heat.

Meanwhile, cook pasta in plenty of boiling, salted water until al dente. Scoop out a cup of pasta cooking water and then drain the pasta. Add the pasta to the skillet and toss to coat with pancetta fat.

In a bowl large enough to toss the cooked pasta, beat eggs and all but 2 tablespoons of cheese. Grind in plenty of black pepper. Add the pasta and cured meat, tossing furiously to keep eggs from scrambling. Then, once the sauce begins to thicken, add a couple of tablespoons of cooking water to loosen. Toss again, divide among warm bowls. Finish the dish with a grating of nutmeg and a little more Parmesan. Serve immediately.

Christine

Ground meat is the gateway to greener pastures

When I first moved to Maine, I took a job teaching cooking classes in the corporate headquarters of jam giant Stonewall Kitchen in Kittery. In my two-year tenure there, I taught over 150 classes and not once did I demonstrate the best way to cook lamb. Not a chop. Not a rack. Not a leg.

Not for lack of trying, mind you. Classes advertised months in advance simply didn't sell if lamb was on offer. The marketing department attributed the lack of interest by average eaters who write off the other red meat as both gamey and expensive.

My argument for repeatedly slipping a little lamb onto the menu is that a proper, polite introduction to some local, ground lamb teaches many eaters to open their minds and palates to a whole range of different—and potentially greener—animal protein available to them.

The cheapest option for cooks looking to buy local, humanely, and sustainably raised meat—beef cattle, goat, lamb, or pigs—is ground meat. It's economical because it typically comprises a mix of less desirable cuts and trim from more expensive cuts taken from the same single animal. This whole animal approach means none of the meat goes to waste, keeping the overall price as low as possible while still covering the farmers' costs. For example, a tenderloin taken from cattle raised its whole life eating organic grass might sell for $35 per pound, while ground meat from the same animal would be under $8 per pound, a much easier sum to swallow.

Yes, the cost of the pastured ground beef (or pork or lamb) is still significantly more than the cost of ground beef (or pork or lamb) from conventionally raised cattle raised in feedlots, fed grain, and given high doses of antibiotics. And so that begs the question, what am I paying for? Is it healthier? Is it cleaner? Is it greener?

Well, that depends. Studies generally come down in favor of organic, pastured meat as being slightly healthier, generally cleaner, and mostly greener. But on any of these fronts, how good the meat is for you or the environment really hinges on the farmers' practices. With the state of meat labeling in the United States in constant flux, you can't always trust what you read on the package. The only way to know whether you're getting what you think you're paying for is to establish a relationship with a farmer and/or trusted butcher and ask if the cows, pigs, or lambs were given any antibiotics, and how they were fed.

From a cook's point of view, a pound of ground meat is one of the most versatile proteins she can have in her freezer. Pastured meat tends to have less fat but a stronger flavor so a small amount can go a long way. It can be shaped in sizes (Pork and Ricotta Meatballs, 98), studded with flavor (Bulgogi Burgers with Quick Pickles and Spicy Mayonnaise, 97), and stretched with interesting fillers and toppers (Scented Sweet Potato, Lamb, and Apple Shepherd's Pie, 101) to accommodate as few or as many eaters as show up at the table.

So pull out a pound of ground, pastured meat from your freezer and politely make your own point regarding just how good it can be.

Breadcrumb stash

Extra burger buns, ground in a food processor and frozen, help stretch future ground meat into more meatballs or add a bit of texture to pasta.

Bulgogi burgers with quick pickles and spicy mayonnaise

Bulgogi is very flavorful Korean beef barbecue, typically made with thinly sliced beef and served with a host of pickled sides. The concept easily transfers to ground beef, giving the traditional all-American burger made with locally sourced ground beef a twist. Gochujang sauce, a Korean fermented chili paste, adds the heat here and can be found in most Asian grocery stores, or replace it with the more popular Sriracha sauce if that's already in your fridge.

Makes 4 burgers

Quick pickles:

- 2 tablespoons sugar
- 2 teaspoon kosher salt
- ½ cup distilled white vinegar
- 2 pickling cucumbers, trimmed and thinly sliced
- 4 radishes, trimmed and thinly sliced

Spicy mayonnaise:

- ½ cup mayonnaise
- 1 to 2 teaspoons gochujang or Sriracha sauce

Burgers:

- 1 pound local grass-fed ground beef
- 2 whole scallions, trimmed and finely chopped
- 1 tablespoon soy sauce
- 1 tablespoon brown sugar
- 1½ teaspoons sesame oil
- 1½ teaspoons finely chopped garlic
- 1½ teaspoons grated ginger
- ½ teaspoon freshly ground black pepper
- 4 hamburger buns
- 4 large pieces of leafy lettuce

To make the pickles, combine ¼ cup hot water with sugar and salt, stirring until dissolved. Add vinegar, cucumbers, and radishes. Refrigerate for 1 hour, but up to 12. Drain and let sit for 10 minutes.

To make the spicy sauce, combine mayonnaise and hot sauce. Refrigerate for 1 hour.

To make the burgers, combine beef, scallions, soy sauce, brown sugar, sesame oil, garlic, ginger, and pepper in a bowl. Form mixture into 4 patties and refrigerate for 1 hour.

Grill the burgers over medium heat (if the heat is too high it will cause the sugar to char) until they reach desired doneness. To assemble burgers, top each bun bottom with lettuce, quick pickles, a cooked burger, and a slathering of spicy mayonnaise.

Pork and ricotta meatballs

My daughter has been on a meatball kick of late, answering, "spaghetti and meatballs" every time I ask for a dinner request. When I comply, I tend to make many meatballs tucking two-thirds in the freezer for future dinners. This recipe, only delicately seasoned so the taste of the local pork comes through, is in the rotation for her favorite dish as well as for Twenty-Minute Meatball Minestrone, *(99)**.*

Makes about 50 golf ball-sized meatballs, enough for
+ Plan-over soup

2 pounds ground pork

1 pound ground mild Italian sausage

1 large bunch of flat-leaf parsley, minced

1 medium onion, grated

3 garlic cloves, grated

1 tablespoon dried oregano

1 tablespoon kosher salt

1 tablespoon cracked black pepper

1½ cups fresh ricotta cheese

3 eggs, lightly beaten

3 cups fresh breadcrumbs

Oil for rolling meatballs

Preheat oven to 375° and line two large baking sheets with silicone mats.

Use your hands to break up the meat into a large mixing bowl. Spread meat around bowl to expose as much surface area as possible. Sprinkle parsley, onion, garlic, oregano, salt, and pepper over meat. Gently mix herbs and spices into meat. Add ricotta, eggs, and breadcrumbs. Fold and gently squeeze mixture until all ingredients are evenly distributed.

Coat your hands with oil and roll 2 to 3 tablespoons of meat into golf ball-sized meatballs. Place them 1 inch apart on prepared baking sheets. Gently slide baking sheets into oven. Bake until meatballs are lightly browned and glistening and have an internal temperature of 165° (20 to 30 minutes). The meatballs can be added to sauce and served with pasta or cooled completely and frozen for future use.

Twenty-minute meatball minestrone

This is a dish that I made from freezer and pantry supplies on a lazy rainy day that included a good book and a nap that bumped up against dinner prep time. If you want to ramp up the flavor, stir in a dollop of Carrot Top Salsa Verde (178).

Serves 4

¾ cup uncooked small shell pasta

1 tablespoon olive oil

1 cup diced onion

1 cup diced carrot

½ cup diced celery

2 tablespoons chopped flat-leaf parsley

2 teaspoons chopped thyme

¼ teaspoon crushed red pepper flakes

4 garlic cloves, chopped

2 cups cooked beans

2 cups chopped canned tomatoes

4 cups chicken stock

12-16 frozen Pork and Ricotta Meatballs, 98

½ teaspoon kosher salt

¼ teaspoon freshly ground black pepper

Grated Parmesan cheese

Cook pasta according to package directions and drain.

While pasta cooks, heat a large saucepan over medium-high heat. Add oil to pan, and swirl to coat. Add onion, carrot, celery, parsley, thyme, red pepper flakes, and garlic. Stirring occasionally, cook for 10 minutes. Add beans, tomatoes, and stock. Bring to a boil. Add meatballs. Reduce heat, and simmer 5 to 7 minutes to reheat the meatballs. Stir in pasta, salt, and black pepper. Cook 1 minute. Serve with grated Parmesan cheese.

Orecchiette with cauliflower, pancetta, and breadcrumbs

Putting a few breadcrumbs in a pasta dish is a common Italian trick for adding texture, taste, and color to a simple sauce. Here I've paired them with peppery cauliflower and salty pancetta. I've included unsalted pepitos—hulled pumpkin seeds—to add a nutty flavor and a shade of green to this pale dish.

Serves 4

Kosher salt

1½ pounds cauliflower, broken into bite sized pieces

1 pound orecchiette

1 cup fresh bread crumbs

½ cup pepitas (hulled pumpkin seeds)

¼ cup good olive oil

3 thick slices of pancetta, cut into ¼-inch cubes.

2 garlic cloves, finely chopped

1 tablespoon lemon

½ cup grated Pecorino, more for serving

½ cup chopped parsley

Ground black pepper

Set a large pot of salted water to boil. Drop in cauliflower and blanch until tender (4 to 5 minutes). Use a slotted spoon to remove cauliflower and set aside. Drop pasta into boiling water and cook until al dente.

In a large skillet, dry toast first the breadcrumbs until they are browned (3 to 4 minutes) and then the pepitas until they start to pop (1 to 2 minutes). Set both ingredients aside.

Pour oil into skillet and fry pancetta pieces until crispy (4 to 5 minutes). Add blanched cauliflower and chopped garlic and sauté until garlic turns golden (1 to 2 minutes).

Drain pasta, reserving one cup of pasta water. Add pasta to skillet. Add ¼ cup pasta water, lemon juice, Pecorino, and parsley. Mix well. Adjust for salt and pepper. Remove from heat and stir in breadcrumbs and pepitas. Serve warm.

Scented sweet potato, lamb, and apple shepherd's pie

This twist on the classic is surprising, beautiful, and a great way to use up leftover mashed sweet and white potatoes.

Serves 8

2 pounds ground local lamb

1 large, sweet onion, peeled and roughly chopped

2 carrots grated

1 3-inch piece of fresh ginger, peeled and roughly chopped

3 garlic cloves, peeled and roughly chopped

1 tablespoon toasted ground cumin

2 teaspoons ground cinnamon

½ teaspoon smoky chili pepper flakes

2 cups chopped tomatoes

2 cups lamb or beef stock

1 tablespoon honey

1 cup chopped dried apples

2 cups mashed sweet potato

1 cup mashed white potato

½ cup plain yogurt

2 tablespoons melted butter

Kosher salt and ground black pepper

1 cup frozen peas

¼ cup of roughly chopped parsley

Toasted cumin seeds (optional)

Brown the lamb, in batches if necessary, in a deep, 12-inch cast iron pan. Drain all but 2 tablespoons of fat from cooked lamb.

Combine onions, carrots, ginger, garlic, and spices in the bowl of a food processor and pulse until all are finely chopped. Add this mixture to skillet and cook until aromatics soften (4 to 5 minutes). Add tomatoes, stock, and honey. Simmer uncovered for 20 minutes. Add dried apples, cover, and simmer for 20 more minutes.

In a large bowl, combine mashed sweet and white potatoes, yogurt, and melted butter. Season with salt and pepper to taste.

Preheat oven to 425°.

Remove skillet from heat. Stir frozen peas and chopped parsley into the filling and season with salt and pepper. Spread potato mixture over filling. If using cumin, sprinkle the toasted seeds over potatoes. Bake until topping begins to brown and filling is hot (35 to 45 minutes). Let pie rest for 10 minutes before serving.

Christine

One healthy local chicken does the trick

My son's 6-foot-5 body plays both basketball and standing bass and requires copious amounts of fuel. My daily dinner budget hovers around $20 to feed the four of us. These two facts of my life don't always jibe—especially when I factor in the cost of sustainably reared proteins.

I can hit the mark on all three points, four, maybe, five times a week with the help of a full repertoire of sausage and pasta dishes; exploration of the cheaper, white, flaky fishes like pollock and cusk; and an ability to stretch a local chicken a country mile, or at least across three meals.

To make the cook-once, eat-three-times chicken policy work, I have to bring home the biggest whole bird in the cooler at the farmers market. Most weeks that sets me back at least $20.

I typically roast a chicken after I've spatchcocked (or butterflied) it and marinated it with lemons and herbs (Lemon and Herb Spatchcock Chicken, 104). I serve the tender white meat and crispy wings with roasted potatoes and a couple of green vegetables.

On day two, I shred the dark meat and use it in Second-day Chicken, Mushroom, and Collard Green Wraps (105).

For meal three, the carcass gets picked clean of meat and the bones recycled in a stockpot with the scraps of onions, celery, and carrots I've collected that week. From there it becomes a favorite—Switch It Up Asian Chicken Noodle Soup (106), a spiced broth served with a plate of the picked chicken meat, lots of noodles and all the Asian fixings eaters need to make the soup just the way they like it.

In *An Everlasting Meal, Cooking with Economy and Grace,* writer Tamar Adler espouses this three-meals-per-chicken rule, too. She prefers simmering a well-salted bird slowly, covered in water with a few staples like carrot peels, onion skins and celery tops, and judiciously employed spices like cinnamon or star anise. This technique, she writes, doesn't intimidate the cook and is gentle on the tender protein.

Adding pieces of turnips, potatoes, leeks, and parsnips to the pot to cook with the bird at the tail end of the simmering, which then get served as side dishes with an herby salsa verde, also makes a richer second-day broth. This liquid gold requires only a few floating ravioli and some cracked black pepper to make a satisfying meal, Adler explains.

Moving beyond the flavorful frugality of pulling off what is essentially classic French chicken *pot-au-feu*, this cooking process consumes just half the energy my own roast-first, boil-later local-chicken-stretching routine does, because it cooks the meat and vegetables and makes the broth in one efficient operation. Yes, you sacrifice the crispy skin of the roasted chicken. On the other hand, Adler points out that you can skim the fat from the top of the pot of broth once it has cooled and use that to sauté vegetables or smear on toast.

By taking either my roasted route or Adler's boiled one, a cook can whittle down the cost of the bird to under $7 per meal. Not a bad price to pay for any chicken, let alone one of this quality and sustainable standing.

Tricky temping

Chicken must be cooked to 165°. If you don't have an instant-read meat thermometer, wait until after the prescribed roasting time, slice the skin between the leg and the breast and peek at the juices. If they run clear, the chicken is done. If they run a cloudy pink, it's not. Roast it 15 minutes longer and run the same check on the other side of the bird.

Lemon and herb spatchcock chicken, page 104

Lemon and herb spatchcock chicken

A spatchcocked (or butterflied) chicken has its backbone removed before it's roasted so the cooking process moves along more quickly. Save the backbone for stock.

Serves 4

+ Plan-over meat for Second-day Chicken, Mushroom, and Collard Green Wraps, 105

1 whole, 4-pound local chicken

¼ cup olive oil

Zest and juice of 2 lemons

4 garlic cloves, roughly chopped

2 tablespoons minced fresh rosemary

2 tablespoons minced fresh thyme

1 tablespoon honey

1 teaspoon kosher salt

1 teaspoon smoky red pepper flakes

Place chicken breast-side down and use a pair of kitchen shears to cut along one side of the backbone. Repeat process along the other side of the backbone. Spread the chicken's ribcage and slice through the white cartilage at the tip of the breastbone. Turn chicken over and press gently to make it flat.

Combine the rest of ingredients in a bowl large enough to hold the chicken. Add chicken and massage marinade into it. Refrigerate overnight.

Preheat oven to 450°.

Remove the chicken from marinade. Spread it out, breast side up on a rimmed baking sheet. Slide tray into oven and roast it for 30 minutes. Lower heat to 350° and roast until a meat thermometer stuck into the thickest part of the breast reads 165° (30 to 40 minutes). Remove pan from oven and rest roasted chicken for 10 minutes before carving it to serve.

Second-day chicken, mushroom, and collard green wraps

These travel well in packed lunches. To make the recipe vegetarian, swap in scrambled eggs for the chicken. Vegans can leave out the protein altogether. Leftover sticky rice works best here if you've got it.

Makes 1 dozen wraps

Wraps:

- 12 long chives (6 inches each) or scallions
- 1 teaspoon vegetable oil
- 6 large shiitake mushrooms, stems removed, caps sliced thinly
- 1 teaspoon rice vinegar
- ¼ teaspoon sugar
- 1 large carrot, grated
- 6 radishes, grated
- 12 large collard green leaves
- ¾ cup cooked rice
- 1 ½ cups shredded cooked chicken
- 24 cilantro leaves

Dipping sauce:

- 2 tablespoons soy sauce
- 1 tablespoon rice wine vinegar
- ½ teaspoon grated ginger
- Splash of hot sauce

Place chives (or scallions) in a bowl and pour boiling water over them. Let sit for 30 seconds, drain and set aside.

Heat oil in small skillet over high heat. Add mushrooms and coat with oil. Cook without stirring until one side of the mushrooms caramelize. Remove mushrooms from pan and set aside.

Combine rice vinegar, sugar, carrots, and radishes in a small bowl. Set aside.

Take 1 collard leaf and cut out any bulky bits of the stem. Press your finger along the leaf's rib to relax it. In the middle of the leaf, place a tablespoon of rice, 2 tablespoons chicken, a few mushrooms, and a good pinch of carrot-radish pickle. Finish with a few cilantro leaves. Fold the sides of the leaf over the filling and roll it up away from you. Secure the wrap with a blanched scallion or chive ribbon. Repeat until all collard leaves are used up.

To make the dipping sauce, combine all ingredients with 3 tablespoons warm water in a small bowl. Serve with wraps.

Switch it up Asian chicken noodle soup

Each place is set with a large piping hot bowl full of noodles in a flavorful, mild broth. A plate of optional ingredients spins on a Lazy Susan set in the middle of the table so everyone can reach it to create their very own version of this soup.

Serves 4

Soup:

- 1 teaspoon vegetable oil
- 4 scallions, white parts halved lengthwise and cut into 1½-inch pieces, green parts thinly sliced
- 1-inch piece fresh ginger, peeled and cut into matchsticks
- 1 garlic clove, peeled and very thinly sliced
- 8 large fresh shiitake mushrooms, stems removed and caps sliced
- 6 cups chicken broth
- 1 tablespoon fish sauce
- 2 cups cooked Asian egg or rice noodles

Mix-ins:

- 1 cup shredded cooked chicken
- 1 cup snow peas, tips and strings removed
- 1 cup mung bean sprouts
- 1 cup baby spinach leaves
- 1 cup shredded carrots
- 1 cup julienned red pepper
- 1 lime sliced into segments
- 1 green serrano chili sliced thinly

Add the oil to a large saucepan over medium-high heat. Stir in scallion whites and ginger, until scallions begin to soften (2 to 3 minutes). Stir in garlic and mushrooms and cook 2 minutes more. Add broth and fish sauce, and bring to a boil. Reduce to a simmer and cook until flavors are well blended (5 to 7 minutes).

Divide cooked noodles among four bowls. Ladle a generous cup of broth over each bowl of noodles. Serve bowls and a large plate holding an assortment of mix-ins.

Honeyed curried chicken

A local beekeeper gave me this simple recipe one fall after his bees had had a particularly busy summer. He makes it with yellow mustard, and I like it with a grainy Dijon, but any prepared mustard will work. Madras is one of the hotter curry powders. In this recipe it registers a three on a scale of five. Adjust as you must. Serve this sweet hot curry over rice and quick stir-fried vegetables.

Serves 4

2 pounds boneless chicken thigh meat, cut into chunks

1 tablespoon Madras curry powder

1 teaspoon kosher salt

½ cup chicken stock

⅓ cup local honey

¼ cup mustard

10 large sprigs of cilantro

2 tablespoons unsalted butter

Preheat oven to 325°.

Toss the chicken with curry powder and salt. In a measuring cup, whisk stock, honey, and mustard. Pinch the leaves from the cilantro sprigs and use a piece of kitchen twine to tie the stems together.

Melt butter in a heavy-bottomed pot with a lid. Add chicken to the pot and cook, stirring occasionally until chicken pieces are browned (3 to 4 minutes). Remove pot from heat, stir in honey mixture. Nestle the bundle of cilantro stems into the sauce.

Cover and bake for 45 minutes. Remove cilantro stems and sprinkle curry with cilantro leaves before serving.

One-pan salmon with spicy creamed greens and tomatoes, page 130

Seafood

Christine

One-fish, two-fish, try a new fish

The term "sustainable seafood" is a loaded one. It's loaded with all the different kinds of the fish in the sea, warming waters, evolving science, multi-tiered regulation, foreign processing facilities, and false marketing tactics.

If you want to ensure there will be fish on offer in markets, grocery stores, and restaurants in the future, you really only have to remember to do two things.

One: Buy American seafood. American fisheries—that term encompasses the fish, the fishermen, and the fleet used to harvest them—are among the most regulated and sustainable in the world. If the seafood was hauled in by an American fisherman, it is as sustainable as it can be. In the frozen aisle, look for the labels that indicate the fish was caught in the USA. If it's in a case, ask the fishmonger where it was caught. If it's an appealing item in a restaurant, don't be embarrassed to ask where it was sourced.

Two: Understand the types of fish you enjoy—flaky and white or meaty and pink—rather than narrowly limiting yourself to one fish in particular. A wider understanding of how each of these types reacts in the pan expands your seafood cookery skills exponentially.

Rather than go to the store armed with a specific recipe and determined to buy a specific fish, walk in and ask the fishmonger what fish is freshest that day, and what has been caught locally.

Once you bring your sustainable seafood home, you've got to know how to store it correctly or it will go off and get wasted. My friend Mollie Sanders Martin has seafood in her blood. She comes from a long line of Portsmouth, New Hampshire fish sellers and has taught me all I know about storing fish correctly. She says it all comes down to keeping it cold and properly wrapped.

When you get your fillets home, take them out of whatever they came in and rinse them well under cold water. Pat them dry with a paper towel and store, covered, in a glass dish, preferably with a glass cover.

Steaks (i.e., tuna, sword, dogfish) need to be treated a little differently or you run the risk of bleaching out the flesh, which won't affect flavor but will turn your fish an unappealing pale color. Give your steaks a very quick dip in cold water, dry them well, and wrap them individually in plastic wrap.

A whole fish should be scaled and gutted. At home, give it a good rinse with cold, running water, pat it with a damp paper towel, wrap it with plastic wrap, and place it in a glass dish, in the coldest part of the fridge.

Mollie is magical, for sure. But not even she can hold fish in the fridge longer than two or three days. So if you're not going to get to cooking your fish after that period of time, better to buy it frozen and keep it so until you are ready to cook it.

Buying frozen fish

Frozen at Sea (FAS) products may be caught, filleted, and frozen aboard the same boat, which is ideal because the freshness is locked in until you are ready to eat it. Avoid "previously frozen" fish, as it was frozen whole on a factory ship and then thawed and reprocessed at a plant ashore, a process that actually unlocks the benefits of freezing fish in the first place. It's best to safely thaw the portions of fish or shellfish you'll need for dinner in the fridge while you're at work.

Rainbow chard-wrapped flaky white fish with lemon, parsley, and hazelnut relish

In Maine, you could make this recipe with cod, haddock, cusk, flounder, hake, or pollock. (If you live elsewhere, ask your fishmonger for a similar type of fish that's locally caught to serve in this dish.) Save the chard stems to make Swiss Chard Stem, Thyme, and Parmesan Cheese Spread Tartines (71).

Serves 4
+ Plan-over chard stems for tartines, 71

2 whole lemons

2 teaspoons kosher salt, divided

¾ teaspoon black pepper, divided

1 teaspoon toasted ground cumin

4 (5-ounce) portions of local flaky white fish fillet

2 tablespoons extra-virgin olive oil

2 teaspoons honey

⅓ cup chopped parsley

¼ cup chopped scallions

¼ cup toasted, chopped hazelnuts

1 tablespoon chopped red chili pepper or ¼ teaspoon red chili pepper flakes

3 tablespoons unsalted butter, melted

4 large (3 inches wide and 6 inches long) rainbow chard leaves, stalks removed

Sea salt, optional

Preheat oven to 400°.

Zest both lemons. In a small bowl, combine 2 teaspoons of zest with 1½ teaspoons salt, ½ teaspoon black pepper, and cumin. Divide the seasoning mixture among the pieces of fish, rubbing it into both top and bottom of the fillets. Set aside.

Segment the lemons, using a sharp knife. Remove all the pith, then, slicing on each side of each membrane, remove the lemon sections. Set aside. Once you have cut out all the segments, squeeze the juice from the lemon "skeleton" over a bowl. Whisk lemon juice with olive oil, honey, ½ teaspoon salt, and ¼ teaspoon black pepper. Gently stir in parsley, scallions, hazelnuts, chiles, and lemon sections. Set aside.

Coat a baking dish with melted butter.

To wrap the fish, lay down one chard leaf, shiny side down, on a cutting board. Use a pastry brush to coat the leaf with butter. In the center of a leaf, place one seasoned fish fillet and wrap ends of the leaf around the fish. Set the bundle, seam side down, in prepared baking dish. Repeat this process with remaining leaves and fish fillets. Brush the top of each bundle with a bit more butter and sprinkle with sea salt. (It seasons and crisps up the chard.)

Bake until the fish is opaque in the center of each bundle (12 to 14 minutes). Serve hot with lemon-parsley relish.

Fish tacos with corn cilantro pesto, red cabbage, and lime

If you are one of those people who thinks cilantro tastes like soap but are still reading about this dish because it sounds interesting, substitute parsley and add more lime juice to the mix when making the pesto. I like to use a flat white flaky fish such as flounder or redfish, the fillets of which get dusted with corn flour, a very finely milled cornmeal.

Serves 4

½ cup corn flour

1 teaspoon chipotle chili powder

½ teaspoon fine sea salt

1½ pounds flaky white fish fillets, cut into 4-inch pieces

Neutral oil for frying fish

8 small corn or flour tortillas, warmed

1 cup Corn Cilantro Pesto (177)

1 cup thinly sliced purple cabbage

Lime wedges for serving

Combine flour with chili powder and salt on a plate. Dredge fish pieces on all sides in the seasoned flour. Set aside.

Add enough oil to a 12-inch frying pan to skim-coat the pan. Place pan over high heat until the oil shimmers. Turn down heat to medium-high and arrange the fish pieces in hot oil. Fry fish until it is slightly browned on one side (4 minutes). Flip pieces and cook until opaque at their centers (2 minutes more for thinner flounder, haddock, and redfish fillets or 4 minutes for thicker pollock, hake, or cod fillets). Set fish on paper bags to drain.

To build the tacos, slather each tortilla with 2 tablespoons of pesto, top with ⅛ of the fish, a tablespoon or so of cabbage and a lime wedge.

Serve immediately.

Blushing New England fish chowder

I once interviewed a seasoned Maine fisherman who said that a good fish chowder has to have a goodly amount of fish in it: "Don't give me one that tastes as if the fish swam through it on his way to another pot." This recipe, while it veers from the traditional New England fish chowder, certainly has enough flaky white fish in it. Choose pollock, which has both light and dark meat, or the freshest American caught option in the fish case.

Serves 4

1 tablespoon olive oil

1 teaspoon butter

2 ounces Spanish chorizo, skin removed and chopped

1 medium, sweet onion, chopped

1 teaspoon smoked paprika

2 teaspoons fresh thyme leaves

1 bay leaf

1 large russet potato, scrubbed and cut into ½-inch cube

3 to 3½ cups seafood stock

1 teaspoon kosher salt

½ teaspoon black pepper

½ cup roasted red peppers, chopped

1½ pounds white flakey fish (such as cod, cusk, haddock, hake, pollock)

½ to 1 cup cream (or half and half, if you must)

2 tablespoons chopped chives (for garnish)

Heat butter and oil in a large saucepan. Add chorizo and cook until it's crisp. Use a slotted spoon to remove chorizo from pan to drain on a paper bag.

Add onion to pot and sauté in fat, until onion is softened. Add paprika, thyme, bay leaf, and potatoes. Add stock to cover the potatoes. Bring chowder to a boil; reduce heat so it simmers until potatoes are soft enough to crush against the side of pot (10 to 15 minutes). Add salt and pepper to taste. Stir in chopped red pepper.

Gently slip whole fish fillets into chowder. Cook on low heat until fish easily breaks in bite sized pieces. When fish is cooked through, remove bay leaf. Add cream, adjusting the amount to your liking.

Ladle hot chowder into bowls, garnish with crispy chorizo and chopped chives.

Crispy whole fish with spicy soy dipping sauce

This recipe is adaptable to whichever whole fresh fish is available at the market. Serving the fish whole with chopsticks in a communal fashion is always fun, but if your eaters aren't up for that, you can fillet the fish after cooking but before serving.

Serves 4

Fish:

- 2 whole fish (about 1½ and 1¾ pounds each), cleaned and scaled
- 1 teaspoon kosher salt
- ¼ teaspoon finely ground black pepper
- 4 lime slices
- 8 sprigs fresh cilantro
- ¼ cup rice flour
- Neutral oil

Sauce:

- ⅓ cup chicken or fish stock
- 3 tablespoons soy sauce
- 2 tablespoons lime juice
- 1 tablespoon fresh orange juice
- 1 tablespoon honey
- 2 teaspoons sesame oil
- ½ teaspoon grated fresh ginger
- ½ teaspoon chili garlic sauce
- 2 scallions, green tops only, thinly sliced
- Cooked rice for serving

Rinse and dry the inside of the fish. Using a sharp knife, make 3 small slits in the flesh of each side of each fish. Sprinkle salt and pepper inside and out of each fish, rubbing the seasoning into the slits in the flesh. Stuff the fish cavity with 2 lime slices and 4 cilantro sprigs. Dust the outside of each fish with flour.

Combine stock, soy sauce, lime and orange juices, honey, sesame oil, ginger, chili garlic sauce, and scallions. Set aside.

Preheat oven to 200°.

Pour enough oil in a large skillet to skim-coat the bottom of the pan. Heat oil on high until it shimmers. Gently place one fish into the pan. Fry until skin is crispy and the flesh inside the slits is opaque (4 to 6 minutes). Flip and fry second side until skin is crispy and flesh is opaque (another 4 to 6 minutes).

Place on a serving platter and stash in the warm oven. Fry the second fish in the same fashion.

Serve fish hot with warm rice and dipping sauce.

Mango and lime marinated meaty fish skewers

The Maine chef who gave me this recipe used dogfish to show how an abundant but underutilized fish in the shark family could be very delicious. If you can't find dogfish, swordfish or sustainable tuna would work well too. The meaty fish fillets are sliced into long, thin pieces that are then threaded onto skewers much like a piece of teriyaki chicken would be skewered. It's best to skewer the fish before marinating it.

Serves 4

1 pound fresh or thawed meaty fish fillets, cut into long ½-inch-thick strips

¼ cup freshly squeezed lime juice

1 ripe mango, peeled, pit removed, and roughly chopped

½ red bell pepper, roughly chopped

½ medium white onion, roughly chopped

1 Thai red chili pepper

2 tablespoons chopped cilantro

2 tablespoons and 1 teaspoon neutral oil

1 teaspoon yellow mustard

1 teaspoon kosher salt

1 teaspoon sugar

A pinch each of turmeric, cinnamon, and allspice powders

Soak four wooden skewers in warm water for 30 minutes. Thread the fish onto soaked skewers.

Combine the other ingredients in a blender and blend until smooth. Pour the marinade over the skewered fish and marinate for 4 hours in the refrigerator, turning once.

Turn on your gas grill, light a charcoal fire, or preheat a grill pan over high heat. When your grill of choice is hot, grill the skewered fish over medium-high heat for 5 to 8 minutes, turning halfway through the cooking process. When the fish is completely opaque, the skewers are done.

Hot smoked salmon kedgeree

At the Kings Head in Bawburgh, Norfolk, England, I ate my first kedgeree, an Anglo-Indian mash-up of spicy rice, smoked fish, fresh shrimp, a soft-cooked egg, and a topping of crispy fried onions. Typically a kedgeree would employ the basmati rice used in Indian food, but I use Thai Jasmine rice left over from making Shrimp and Shredded Kale, Fennel, and Carrot Stir-fry (118).

Serves 2-4

5 tablespoons vegetable oil

1 large medium onion, halved and thinly sliced plus 1 medium onion, chopped

Kosher salt

2 large local eggs

2 tablespoons curry powder

4 split cardamom pods

1 cinnamon stick, broken into pieces

1 dried red chili pepper

¼ pound raw shrimp

3 cups cooked Jasmine rice

⅔ cup frozen peas

½ teaspoon turmeric

2 tablespoons unsalted butter

¼ pound hot-smoked salmon

2 tablespoons chopped cilantro

2 wedges of lime

To crisp the onions, heat 2 tablespoons of the oil in a large, deep frying pan. Add the sliced onions and a pinch of salt and cook over medium heat, stirring occasionally, until they are deeply golden, 15 minutes. Spread on a flattened paper bag to crisp. Set aside.

Meanwhile, put the eggs in a small saucepan, cover with cold water and bring the water to a boil. Let the water boil for 6 minutes. Remove the pan from the heat and plunge the eggs into cold water. Peel the eggs and quarter them.

To make the kedgeree, heat the remaining 3 tablespoons oil in the frying pan over medium-high heat. Add chopped onions, curry, cardamom, cinnamon, and chili pepper and cook, stirring often, until onion is soft and golden (5 to 7 minutes). Add shrimp and cook for 2 minutes. Add cooked rice, peas, turmeric, and ⅓ cup water. Stir to coat the rice. Cook for 2 minutes. When rice is warmed through, remove the pan from the heat and stir in butter. Break the smoked fish into pieces and stir them into the rice.

To serve, stir the cilantro into the rice. Taste and add salt if necessary. Nestle the egg quarters into the rice and scatter the crispy onions on top. Serve with lime wedges.

Smoked fish

Hot smoked fish (a dish that uses fattier fish like salmon, trout, mackerel, and bluefish) is marinated, cured for four hours, and fully cooked (to 140°) with heated wood smoke. You can hot smoke your own fish, but I find it in a grocery store right near the cold smoked salmon. Higher end markets might carry fish that was smoked in-house at the seafood counter. Because hot smoked salmon is smoky and silky, you can get away with serving less. Lox refers to salmon, in particular, that has been cured in a salt-sugar rub or brine and is not smoked at all.

Shrimp and shredded kale, fennel, and carrot stir-fry

This dish takes Plan-over shredded vegetables (Apple, Carrot, and Kale Slaw, 45), puts them in a sauté pan with shrimp, garlic, ginger, and cream, and serves over rice for a 20-minute meal.

Serves 4 plus 3 cups of
+ Plan-over rice for kedgeree, 117

2½ cups Jasmine rice

2 tablespoons neutral oil

1 tablespoon finely chopped fresh ginger

1 tablespoon finely chopped lemongrass

1 tablespoon finely chopped garlic

1 tablespoon finely chopped seeded Thai bird or serrano chili (optional)

1 pound shrimp, peeled and deveined

3 cups shredded kale, fennel, and carrots

1 cup well-shaken unsweetened coconut milk

3-4 tablespoons fresh lime juice

1 tablespoon fish sauce

¼ cup chopped fresh mint

Place rice in a colander and rinse. Add rinsed rice to a 4-quart pot with 4 cups water. Place pot over medium-high heat and bring to a boil. Cover pot. Let boil for 1 minute. Turn off heat and let rice steam, untouched for 20 minutes. After steaming, fluff rice with a fork.

To make the stir-fry, heat oil in a 12-inch skillet over medium-high heat until shimmering. Add ginger, lemongrass, garlic, and chili (if using). Cook, stirring constantly, until fragrant (30 seconds). Add shrimp and cook, stirring, until opaque on the outside and partially cooked (2 minutes). Stir in vegetables and cook for 1 minute. Stir in the coconut milk, lime juice, and fish sauce and cook, stirring, until the shrimp are opaque in the center (1 minute more).

Top four portions of rice with shrimp and vegetables with remaining sauce, and garnish with mint. Serve hot.

Buying shrimp

Buying frozen, wild, shell-on, American shrimp, typically from the South Atlantic or Gulf of Mexico, is always a greener choice than any imported products due to concerns over both fishing and labor practices. Peeling and deveining them are worth the effort. Also, to keep portion size in check and minimize waste, look for Individually Quick Frozen (IQF) shrimp as they don't clump in the package so you can thaw out only what you need.

Ruby red grapefruit and chili glazed grilled scallops

The spicy bittersweet flavor of this glaze helps highlight the sweetness of the scallops. This dish can be easily quartered for a solo supper or doubled for a dinner party.

Serves 4

16-20 large dry-packed sea scallops

1 ruby red grapefruit

2 tablespoons plus one teaspoon honey

1 tablespoon olive oil

1 teaspoon champagne vinegar

1 garlic clove, minced

1 teaspoon minced Fresno and/or Serrano chili

Skewers (presoak wooden skewers in warm water for 30 minutes)

Kosher salt and black pepper

Neutral oil

4 cups arugula

Remove the crescent-shaped tendon (aka the "foot") from the side of each scallop. Use a paper towel to pat dry scallops and place them on a baking rack sitting inside a baking sheet. Refrigerate scallops until just before grilling.

In a small, non-reactive saucepan, combine 1 teaspoon of zest and all of the juice (⅔ cup) from one grapefruit, honey, olive oil, vinegar, and minced garlic. Simmer the mixture over medium heat until it thickens slightly into a glaze (3 to 4 minutes). Stir in minced chili. Set aside.

Turn grill to high and heat grates with cover closed. Open the cover and use a steel brush to completely clean the grates. Cover to reheat grates until piping hot (2 to 3 more minutes).

Remove the scallops from refrigerator; slide scallops on each skewer so the flat sides are all aligned perpendicular to the skewer; and, season with salt and pepper.

Liberally dampen a wad of paper towel with oil. Grab the wad with a pair of tongs, and rub the towels along the grates to grease them well. Repeat this process 3 times. Turn heat to medium-high. Place skewered scallops on one side of the grill at an angle so you will get diagonal grill marks.

Cook skewers 4 minutes, turn and cook for 2 minutes more. Brush glaze over the scallops. Keep scallops on heat until just cooked through: barely opaque in the middle. If unsure, cut one in half to check.

To serve, arrange arugula on a platter or individual plates, top with scallops, and drizzle the glaze over the top. Serve immediately.

Bigger is better

When shopping for scallops, buy the biggest, dry-packed scallops on offer. The bigger the sea scallop, the sweeter it will be. These big boys are more forgiving on the grill, meaning they won't slip from raw to rubber as quickly as smaller ones do or fall through the grates. A dry-packed scallop is not pumped full of watery preservatives, which plump them up in the case but get released when they are cooked, leaving the scallop deflated and chewy.

Hot smoked trout, soba, and Asian greens salad

This is a recipe I recreated after eating one like it at the Two Fat Ladies seafood restaurant in Glasgow, Scotland. There are many Asian greens available at farmers markets at various times of the year—bok choy, baby bok, tat soi, gai lan, Napa cabbage, and Yau Choy, to name a few—but they are all pretty much like cabbage and just need to be chopped to mix in with this dish. Buy whatever looks best.

Serves 4

Juice of one lemon

1/4 cup soy sauce

3 tablespoons mirin (Japanese sweet cooking wine)

2 teaspoons finely grated ginger

2 teaspoons brown sugar

1 teaspoon toasted sesame oil

2/3 cup warm water, more if necessary

12 ounces cooked Soba buckwheat noodles

2 cups chopped Asian greens

8 ounces hot smoked trout, skin removed

Toasted sesame seeds

1 small red chili, thinly sliced

Whisk lemon juice, soy sauce, mirin, ginger, sugar, and sesame oil. Add water to desired strength. You want this to be somewhat thin as it's more of a broth than a dressing. Set aside.

Divide noodles into 4 wide bowls. Pour 1 tablespoon of dressing over each bowl of noodles and mix well.

Divide Asian greens among the bowls and mix with the dressed noodles. Break the fish into bite-sized pieces and distribute the pieces on top of the salads.

Drizzle the remaining dressing across the salad bowls, sprinkle each with toasted sesame seeds and sliced chiles, and serve.

DIY noodles differ from homemade pasta in that they require neither eggs nor a specialty pasta rolling machine. All you need is flour, hot water and a rolling pin.

To make interesting noodles combine 1 cup of flavorful flour (acorn, buckwheat, barley, chickpea, coconut, rye or sorghum) and 1 cup predictable workhorse flour (all-purpose, 00, spelt, or einkorn all-purpose) in a bowl. Stir in 3/4 cup hot water and knead the dough in the bowl with your hands to get a rough, slightly crumbly dough. Turn dough out onto a clean surface and knead until smooth (3 to 4 minutes). If the dough cracks at all, add more water to it by kneading it with wet hands. Once the dough is smooth, shape it into a flat rectangle. Sprinkle the work surface and the top of the dough with a dry flour (semolina or rice) to prevent it sticking to the counter or

the rolling pin. Roll the dough from the center of the rectangle outward, shaping the edges as you go until it is 1⁄16-inch thick. Spread a generous handful of dry flour over the dough. Fold the top third of the dough down over the middle of the rectangle and sprinkle the top with more dry flour. Fold the bottom third of the dough upwards, like you would fold a letter, and coat the top one last time with dry flour. Work your way across the folded dough, cutting into 2⁄3-inch strips with a sharp knife. Toss the cut noodles with a little more semolina or rice flour so they don't stick together. At this point, you can freeze the noodles for up to three months.

Christine

Sweet, succulent bi-valves provide an ecosystem service

I'd never eaten as many bi-valves—clams, oysters, and mussels—as I have since moving to Maine. I like them raw, broiled, fried, and steamed in all sorts of interesting liquids. Bring them on!

It's not just me. Friends who visit from all the other places I've lived—Western Massachusetts, Connecticut, New Jersey, Pennsylvania, England and, yes, even France—clamor for a wide sampling of Maine oysters. I always oblige. But after shucking literally hundreds of Bagaduce, Flying Point, Glidden Point, John's River, Nonesuch, North Haven, Taunton Bay, and Pemaquid oysters, I had to ask myself, just how many oysters is too many oysters to pull out of the Gulf of Maine to be ecologically sound?

That's a tough question, said Dana Morse, a scientist with Maine Sea Grant and University of Maine Cooperative Extension. The vast majority of oysters that make their way onto dinner plates in the United States are farmed, as over 80 percent of the world's wild oyster beds have been eaten or destroyed by pollution and/or warming waters. According to the Maine Department of Marine Resources, the agency that grants permits for all aquaculture sites, Maine has over 70 oyster farms. The number grows every year.

In recent years, Morse says "wild" oysters have been showing up on the shorelines again—most probably products of successful spawns from the farmed oysters. In that case, the farms have helped rebuild wild oyster beds with what Morse called "naturalized" or feral oysters.

Mark Green, a Saint Joseph College oceanography professor and owner of Basket Island Oyster Company in Casco Bay who harvests a couple hundred thousand oysters per year, says that's a good thing. He explains that oysters, mussels, and clams play into marine life sustainability because they provide an ecosystem service. As filter feeders, they eat phytoplankton and remove nitrogen and phosphorous from the ecosystem, thereby improving the quality of water for the fish that swim in it.

Bits about bi-valves

Bi-valves need to breathe. So store them in the refrigerator in a roomy glass or metal container draped with a damp cloth. Only rinse them just before preparing them to eat. Bi-valves should be tight lipped. Only buy ones that are closed. They may open while in storage, but should close again immediately when you tap on the shell. If they don't, discard.

Clams with grains and baby kale

This recipe was adapted from one I had at the Palace Diner in Biddeford, Maine, made with mahogany clams, which are bigger and a bit more metallic tasting than the smaller littlenecks I suggest here. Littlenecks are more readily available outside of Maine.

Serves 4

2 tablespoons olive oil

½ cup chopped fennel

¼ cup minced shallots

2 garlic cloves, crushed

½ teaspoon whole fennel seeds

1 cup clam juice

4 dozen littleneck clams, scrubbed

2 cups cooked, warm farro, wheat berries, barley, or rye berries

½ cup heavy cream

Kosher salt and white pepper

4 cups washed baby kale leaves

Chili oil

In a pot large enough to hold all of the clams, heat 2 tablespoons olive oil over medium heat. Add chopped fennel and shallots. Cook, stirring until soft (3 to 4 minutes). Add garlic and fennel seeds and cook for 1 minute more. Add clam juice and bring to a steady simmer. Carefully scatter the clams into the pot and cover. Cook until clams have opened (5 to 7 minutes). Discard any unopened clams. Divide warm farro and cooked clams among warmed bowls.

Return pot to stove, add cream, and bring to a simmer over low heat. Turn off heat, season with salt and white pepper, and fold in the baby kale leaves. Spoon kale and sauce over clams. Finish each bowl with a swirl of chili oil.

Cranberry, ginger, and apple mignonette for oysters

I collaborated on this recipe with oyster farmer friend Abigail Carroll of Nonesuch Oyster Company. We were chatting online when she mentioned that she'd love to create a recipe for the holidays that paired oysters and cranberries. A mignonette is a classic French condiment served with raw oysters. I consulted classic French cookbooks and reference guides that help pair flavors, and we settled on cranberry and ginger-infused vinegar and apples as a festive topper for oysters on the half shell.

Makes ¼ cup mignonette
+ Plan-over 1¼ cups of infused vinegar to spare

2 cups white balsamic vinegar

1 cup fresh or frozen cranberries, roughly chopped

1-inch piece fresh ginger, sliced into ¼-inch medallions

2 tablespoons minced apple

2 tablespoons minced shallot

Freshly ground black pepper

24 raw oysters, shucked and presented on the half-shell

Combine the vinegar, cranberries, and ginger slices in a small pan. Place the mixture over medium heat until it begins to simmer. Simmer for 5 minutes. Remove from heat, let cool to room temperature, and strain. Reserve berries and ginger for your next batch of cranberry sauce. Pour infused vinegar into a jar with a lid. Vinegar can be stored at room temperature for 2 months.

In a small bowl, combine ½ cup cranberry-ginger vinegar with the apples, shallots and black pepper to taste.

Serve with chilled raw oysters on the half-shell.

Cranberry
Vinegar

Smoky mussels with thyme and tomatoes

Mussels are a great weeknight staple because they are sustainable, widely available, keep in the refrigerator, and cook up quickly in one pot.

Serves 4

4 pounds fresh mussels

2 tablespoons olive oil

½ cup chopped onion

2 tablespoons roughly chopped garlic

6 sprigs thyme

2 teaspoons smoked paprika

2 cups dry white wine

2 cups peeled, diced, canned tomatoes

1 tablespoon roughly chopped capers

1 tablespoon roughly chopped garlic

½ cup cream (optional)

2 tablespoons chopped parsley

Crusty bread, for serving

Put the mussels in a colander and rinse well with cold water, discarding any with cracked shells or open ones that don't close quickly when you tap them on a hard surface. Pull off any attached beards.

Heat the oil over medium-high heat in a pot large enough to hold the mussels. Add onions and cook until translucent (4 minutes). Add garlic, thyme, and paprika and cook 1 minute more. Add wine, tomatoes, capers, second measure of garlic, and mussels. Give the mussels a good stir. Cover and cook until the mussels have opened completely (6 to 8 minutes).

Discard any mussels that have not opened. Stir in the cream, if using. Cover and let sit for 3 minutes. Sprinkle with parsley. Serve these from the pot with plenty of crusty bread for soaking up the sauce.

Christine

Can obsolete ideas about sardines, seaweed, and farmed salmon

Sardines, seaweed, and farmed salmon have suffered from one "ewww" factor or another. Your grandmother ate sardines because she had to. You avoided stepping on seaweed at the beach. And salmon farming was a polluting venture in the early years. But times have changed and these three power seafoods deserve a spot in your rotation.

Wild Atlantic herring—one of 20 species worldwide that get called "sardines"—are inexpensive, flavorful, and plentiful. But despite all these excellent reasons to eat them, most sardines in Maine get used for lobster bait. Chef Chris Gould, owner of Central Provisions in Portland, is doing his part to change that trend. He salts summer sardines to sock away for winter use and grills them fresh to top crostini with spicy house-made harissa and local radishes (Sardine, Harissa, and Radish Bruschetta, 131). Reasonably priced on his menu, the exotically spiced sardines have sold out every time.

Seaweed is abundant and regenerates without the help of fertilizers or pesticides—or watering, for that matter. If we don't pollute the intertidal zones in which it flourishes, it can provide much-needed nutrients for many people. The ones most harvested in the United States and dried for culinary use are reddish-purple dulse,

golden-brown kelp, thin green sea lettuce, and laver, which most people know as nori (the stuff sushi rolls are wrapped in).

Sea vegetables—the trendy term for seaweed—are a mealtime staple for marine educator Carol Steingart in Wells. She steeps a culinary seaweed blend to use as a starter for miso soups and lentil stews. She sprinkles flakes into noodle and rice dishes. She sticks a two-inch piece of dark green kelp in a pot of beans to help soften their skins, making them more digestible, and hides bits in chocolate brownie batter. The best ways to introduce eaters to seaweed is to swap the bacon in a BLT for a couple of pieces of pan-fried dulse (Read tip DLT technique, 131). Try it—it works.

Since my family loves salmon, I'm often faced with the choice between wild Alaskan salmon and the variety farmed here on the East Coast. Which is greener? The wild variety swam with lots of other fish in its natural habitat, eating its rightful prey, and offers the strongest salmon flavor. But as best practices emerge, "regular old farmed salmon" has become more sustainable than it was in the past.

Farmed salmon today eat meals formulated with 28 percent forage fish like herring and mackerel (down from 95 percent). The rest of their food comes from sustainably farmed plant proteins. This reformulation lessens the burden that salmon farming places on wild fisheries. Antibiotic use has also dropped off dramatically, since all young salmon are vaccinated against the bacteria they'll likely encounter before being placed into the ocean.

In Maine, adequate flushing (when the waves and currents disperse waste from full fish pens) is required in the permitting of farm sites. Further, one-third of Maine's 25 permitted salmon farming sites sit fallow each year allowing the sites to flush completely.

If greener is your goal, ask for salmon farmed with these best practices when you shop.

Skinning pink-fleshed fish

Place the side of salmon, arctic char, or steelhead trout skin side up under the broiler so the skin chars and bubbles (3 to 5 minutes). Peel off the skin with a pair of tongs. Flip it to finish broiling and serve.

One-pan salmon with spicy creamed greens and tomatoes

This recipe works well with all types of salmon, wild-caught or farmed. Serve the fish with crusty bread.

Serves 4

4 (5-ounce) skinless salmon fillets

Kosher salt and black pepper

2 tablespoons olive oil

½ cup chopped sweet onion, such as Vidalia

2 garlic cloves, thinly sliced

½ teaspoon red pepper flakes

8 cups chopped greens (spinach, kale, mustard greens, or Swiss chard)

1 cup chopped tomatoes

¼ cup vegetable, seafood, or chicken stock

½ cup cream

Season the fillets with salt and pepper. Heat 1 tablespoon oil in large, heavy skillet over high heat until very hot. Place the salmon, seasoned-side down, into hot pan to sear for 3 to 4 minutes. Remove the fish from the pan to a plate. The fillets will not yet be cooked through.

Lower the heat to medium. Add the remaining 1 tablespoon oil. Add onions and sauté until they start to soften (4 minutes). Add garlic and red pepper flakes. Cook for 1 minute.

Add the greens and ½ teaspoon salt. Use a pair of tongs to turn the greens in the oil. Add tomatoes, stock, and cream. Stir to combine.

Nestle the salmon fillets, seared side up, into the greens. Cover and cook salmon until medium rare (5 minutes) or well done (10 minutes).

Sardine, harissa, and radish bruschetta

Chef Chris Gould uses fresh grilled sardines, makes his own harissa (a sweet and spicy hot chili paste used in North African cooking), and adds an exotic spice mixture that includes cocoa nibs, Urfa pepper, and sumac. This recipe is updated for the home cook and uses canned fancy (but sustainably sourced) sardines, commercial harissa, and za'atar, an easier to find Middle Eastern spice mix. I prefer boneless sardines but if you don't mind the bones and want the calcium, go ahead and use whole sardines.

Makes 4 bruschetta

2 tablespoons cornmeal

2 teaspoons za'atar

1 can boneless smoked sardines packed in olive oil, drained, split, and patted dry (8 fillets)

4 slices sourdough bread

3 tablespoons olive oil plus extra for bread

1 large garlic clove, peeled and sliced in half

4-8 teaspoons harissa

2 fresh radishes, thinly sliced

1 lemon, zest removed and fruit cut into wedges

2 tablespoons sliced chives

Coarse sea salt

Combine cornmeal and za'atar in a shallow bowl. Toss sardines in cornmeal mixture until coated. Shake off excess. Set aside.

Preheat grill pan on a hot burner. Liberally brush slices of bread with olive oil. Place bread, oil-side down, on grill until bread is toasted and has solid grill marks (3 to 4 minutes). Remove bread from grill and rub the bread with halved garlic clove. Slather 1 to 2 teaspoons of harissa (based on desired spice level) on each bruschetta.

Pour 3 tablespoons of olive oil in a skillet over medium-high heat. Fry sardines until golden brown and crisp, 2 minutes per side. Place two fillets on each bruschetta. Top each with radishes and a squeeze of lemon. Garnish with chopped chives, lemon zest, and sea salt.

DLT technique

The best way to demonstrate the possibility of this sandwich to a BLT lover is to have them make the sandwich exactly the way they would if bacon were in the mix. Use the exact bread, their favorite tomato and lettuce, and whichever mayonnaise they prefer. To give dried dulse, which has a thin leathery feel, the right texture and smoky salty flavor as bacon, smooth out 2 to 3 long pieces, and lay them in a hot, dry skillet. Use a spatula to hold the dulse flat against the pan as it crisps up and turns from a deep burgundy to a reddish brown color. Flip the dulse once to crisp up the other side. Assemble the sandwich as you would for a BLT, slice, and serve.

Lavender lemon posset with candied lemon peel, page 152

Sweets & snacks

Christine

Local cheese is greener cheese

Because I am a turophile, I always bring a cheese plate to the neighborhood potluck. So when I see reports coming out of Washington, D.C., telling me cheese has the third largest carbon footprint among all sources of protein—it stands behind beef (No. 2) and lamb (No. 1)—my heart sinks as I look for the loophole in the data.

Several factors combine to make the commercial cheese industry a major agricultural contributor to greenhouse gas emissions. Cows produce methane, transporting grain and feed means more time spent burning fossil fuels, and there is significant energy expended turning one gallon of milk into roughly one pound of cheese. Plus, when you buy imported cheese, you factor in the environmental costs of shipping a wheel from, say, France to the U.S.

Obviously, buying local cheese is one way to cut down on transportation-related emissions. So that is loophole number one. Maine Cheese Guild President Eric Rector, cheesemaker and owner of the Monroe Cheese Studio, says there are questions a cheese eater can ask of suppliers to find more loopholes and buy greener cheese.

Question the source of the cheesemaker's raw material—the milk. Farmstead cheese is made from milk produced on the same farm where the cheese is made. Barring that possibility, closer is better. Rector raises beef cattle, so he sources raw milk for his British-style blue, natural rind Gouda-style, and cave-aged cheeses from a farmer who raises Jerseys eight miles down the road.

Next, ask what the animals ate. "There is no set definition for 'grass-based' milk production," Rector says. Most local dairy animals whose milk ends up in cheese are pastured in summer and are fed hay in winter, but there is most likely a little grain in the mix as well. Rector suggested asking how much grain the cows are fed and where it comes from, noting that grain shipped from Russia carries a heavy emissions burden.

Rector contends the best place to buy local cheese is at farmers markets because they give producers the best margin, making their businesses more sustainable. That said, there are many retailers that offer local cheeses and asking for them increases the likelihood that there will be more on offer in the future.

Serving cheeses at room temperature brings out their flavors, and pairing them with chutney (Double Cranberry and Ginger Multi-grain Chutney, 136) made from local ingredients and DIY crackers (Kathy's Crackers, 137) that bypass commercial packaging provide nice counterpoints. This combination will indulge your love of cheese without all the carbon guilt.

Cheese board rules

Three cheeses to a board. Buy two ounces of cheese for each eater including: hard cheese (like a cheddar), stinky cheese (like a blue), and bloomy-rind cheese (like Camembert) made from a variety of milks (goat, sheep, and cow). Serve cheese at room temperature.

Kathy's multi-grain crackers, page 137

Double cranberry and ginger chutney

This recipe is adapted from one I found in a Cornish, New Hampshire community cookbook. Tart cranberries and spicy ginger combine for a nice cheese plate condiment.

Makes 2 cups or 2, ½-pint jars

1 medium lemon

12 ounces fresh cranberries (3 cups)

½ cup unsweetened dried cranberries

1½ cups raw sugar

½ cup diced crystallized ginger

⅓ cup finely chopped onion

1 garlic clove, minced

1 cinnamon stick

1 teaspoon mustard seeds

½ teaspoon kosher salt

Zest the lemon. Using a small, sharp paring knife, cut away and compost the thick white pith. Cut lemon crosswise in half and pick out seeds. Dice lemon into ¼-inch pieces.

In a nonreactive medium saucepan, combine cranberries, diced lemon and zest, sugar, ginger, onion, garlic, cinnamon stick, mustard seeds, and salt. Add ¼ cup water. Bring to boil over medium heat, stirring often to help dissolve sugar. Reduce heat to low and simmer until chutney is thick and cranberries have burst (10 to 15 minutes). Cool completely. Remove cinnamon stick just before serving at room temperature.

The chutney can be covered tightly and refrigerated. Alternatively, hot chutney can be poured into prepared ½-pint jars and processed in a hot water bath for 10 minutes to be shelf-stable.

Kathy's multi-grain crackers

Once you make these crackers, you won't go back to the pre-packaged kind. This recipe comes from Kathy Heye who, with her best friend, Deede Montgomery, run Bessie's Farm Goods, a charming general store in Freeport, Maine. If you find yourself in town, swing by their store, be enveloped by the pure joy they take in selling all the local products they love, and walk out with either Kathy's crackers or Deede's killer coffee cake.

Makes 48 crackers, depending how you cut them

3 cups old-fashioned rolled oats

2 cups unbleached all-purpose flour

1 cup wheat germ

¾ cup neutral oil

⅓ cup brown sugar

1 teaspoon kosher salt, more for sprinkling

Preheat oven to 350°.

Combine all ingredients with 1 cup water in a bowl. Mix together to form a dough. Press dough into 2 ungreased rimmed 11 by 17-inch sheet pans. Sprinkle lightly with salt. Cut dough into cracker-sized rectangles or triangles.

Bake for 30 minutes. At the 20-minute mark, watch for browning crackers around the edge of the pan. As individual crackers brown, take them out of the oven and cool on a rack. As you pull crackers from around the edges, spread remaining ones around the pan so they brown and crisp evenly.

Cool crackers before storing in airtight containers for up to 2 weeks.

Double cranberry and
ginger chutney, page 136

Strawberries and cream fairy cakes

Fairy cakes are just modestly sized cupcakes with a more magical name. The cake part of this recipe is based on one pulled from a 1950 edition of Betty Crocker's picture cookbook, first owned by my husband's grandmother, Madalen, who was a splendid cake maker. Fresh, soft cheeses like mascarpone, quark, and fromage blanc are some of the easiest to buy locally and the more recipes one has to use them, the better.

Makes 12 fairy cakes

Cakes:

- 1½ cups cake flour
- 1 cup sugar
- 2 teaspoons baking powder
- ½ teaspoon salt
- ⅓ cup softened, unsalted butter
- ⅔ cup buttermilk
- 1 teaspoon vanilla extract
- 1 egg

Filling and frosting:

- 1 cup heavy cream
- ½ cup mascarpone, quark, or fromage blanc cheese
- 1 tablespoon confectioners' sugar
- ¼ cup strawberry preserves
- ¼ cup halved local strawberries

Preheat oven to 350°. Line a 12-cup cupcake tin with reusable silicone liners or grease with a generous amount of butter.

Whisk flour, sugar, baking powder, and salt in the bowl of a stand mixer or in a medium sized bowl. Add butter, ⅓ cup buttermilk, and vanilla. Beat on medium speed for 2 minutes. Add egg and remaining ⅓ cup buttermilk. Beat 2 minutes more. Fill each cup with a scant ¼ cup batter.

Bake until fairy cakes are golden and springy to the touch (18 to 20 minutes). Remove from oven and cool completely.

To make the filling and frosting, beat cream to very soft peaks. Add mascarpone, quark, or fromage blanc and beat 30 seconds more. Remove two-thirds of the mixture to a second bowl and stir in confectioners' sugar. Gently fold preserves into remaining unsweetened cream-cheese mixture.

With a melon baller, scoop out the center of each cupcake base and set aside. Fill cavities with strawberry cream mixture and plug holes with reserved cake pieces. Frost each fairy cake with sweetened whipped cream. Decorate with halved strawberries.

Easier-than-you-think soft pretzels

Easier-than-you-think pretzels are still a 3-hour project, but half of that time is waiting for the dough to rise. Barley malt syrup is an unrefined sweetener produced from sprouted malted barley. It both sweetens the pretzels and gives them a deep brown color. If you don't have it, use honey in the dough and molasses in the water bath. For an interesting twist, substitute 1 cup pickle brine for the water prescribed for the dough.

Makes 8 pretzels

1 cup warm water

1 package of active dry yeast

Pinch of sugar

2 cups white whole wheat flour, more for kneading

1 cup rye flour

2 tablespoons barley malt syrup, divided

1½ teaspoons kosher salt

Neutral oil

¼ cup baking soda

1 large egg, whisked with 2 tablespoons warm water

Coarse sea salt

Whisk warm water, yeast, and a pinch of sugar in a large bowl. Let it stand for a few minutes. Add flours, 1 tablespoon barley syrup, and salt. Stir into a shaggy dough with a wooden spoon or whisk.

Turn the dough out onto a clean surface dusted with flour. Knead dough until it's slightly tacky and holds a ball shape (5 to 7 minutes). Rinse and dry the bowl. Coat it with oil. Place dough in the prepared bowl, cover and let it rise for an hour in a warm place (between 70 and 80 degrees) until it has doubled in size. Turn risen dough out onto a clean surface dusted with flour. Divide it into eight equal pieces and cover with a damp cloth.

To shape the pretzels, use your palms to roll one piece of dough into a long rope (18 inches long). Position the rope in a U-shape with the ends facing you. Cross the ends over each other twice to make a twist, and fold the twist back down over the bottom loop. Gently press down where the ends meet the curve of the U to seal.

Set the pretzel on a silicone lined baking sheet. Repeat process with remaining portions of dough. Let formed pretzels rise for 20 minutes.

Preheat oven to 450°. Place a rack in middle of oven.

Pour 8 cups of water into a large, deep pot and set over high heat. When water boils, add remaining tablespoon barley syrup and baking soda. Stir to dissolve, making sure the pot doesn't boil over. Adjust heat so water simmers.

Use a slotted spoon to lower 2 pretzels into water bath. Simmer for 30 seconds as they get puckered and doughy looking. Remove from water to rest on baking sheet. Repeat process with remaining pretzels.

You can freeze the pretzels at this juncture. If you aren't going to eat them all now, this is the best way to preserve them for future use.

Brush boiled pretzels with egg wash and sprinkle with salt. Bake pretzels until they are deeply browned and glossy (12 to 15 minutes from fresh, 18 to 20 minutes from frozen).

Cool slightly and serve.

Beer cheese spread

My friend Ali and I produce pop-up restaurants once in a while. She worked up this recipe to serve with warm, Easier-than-you-think Soft Pretzels (140) at an event featuring American comfort food. We used Allagash's Confluence, a local limited edition strong golden ale, but any IPA would work well.

Makes 2½ cups

2 tablespoons unsalted butter

1 cup finely chopped onions

12 ounces shredded sharp cheddar cheese

2 teaspoons hot sauce

1 teaspoon coarse Dijon mustard

1 teaspoon Worcestershire sauce

6 ounces beer

½ teaspoon fresh thyme leaves

Kosher salt and black pepper

Melt butter over medium low heat in a heavy skillet. Stir in onions and cook slowly until golden brown and soft (12 to 15 minutes). Set aside to cool.

Combine cheese, hot sauce, mustard, and Worcestershire sauce in the bowl of a food processor. Pulse until mixture is smooth and creamy. Scrape down the bowl. With processor running, slowly add beer. Add caramelized onions and pulse to combine. Stir in thyme. Season to taste with salt and pepper.

Serve immediately or store covered in refrigerator for a week.

Candied mixed peppers

This recipe is adapted from one my friend Cathy Barrow introduced me to years ago when she was teaching me how to make fresh cheese. The base recipe used only jalepeños and regular granulated sugar. I am a total spice wimp so I mix in some sweet little peppers alongside the hot ones, and I like the deeper sweetness honey and raw sugar give the finished condiment. Like Cathy, I serve these sweet hot peppers on crackers slathered with homemade ricotta. It also goes really well with a local goat, German quark, or French fromage blanc cheese. Triple the batch if you want to process some in a water bath to be shelf-stable. They make festive holiday gifts.

Makes 2½ cups or 5, ½-pint jars

1 cup apple cider vinegar

1 cup honey

¾ cups raw sugar

1 teaspoon minced garlic

¼ teaspoon celery seed

1 pound (¼-inch-thick) slices of mixed hot and sweet peppers such as jalapeños, Fresnos, Lipstick and Hungarian wax

Before you start the recipe, have clean jars ready to house the finished peppers.

Combine the vinegar, honey, sugar, garlic, and celery seed in a medium saucepan. Bring it to a boil over medium heat. Stir so that the sugar dissolves. Add sliced peppers. Bring mixture back to a boil. Cook for 5 minutes.

Remove pan from the heat, use a slotted spoon to transfer the peppers into clean jars. Return the pan with the syrup to the stove, simmer the syrup over medium heat until it thickens to the viscosity of room-temperature maple syrup. Carefully pour the syrup into the jars with the peppers. Cover, cool and store in the refrigerator.

Christine

Ethical, sustainably produced chocolate you can feel good about

The Maine Chocolatier Kate Shaffer believes that since chocolate makes most of us smile, it's only just that we choose chocolate products that are sourced ethically and sustainably.

I couldn't agree more. But knowing which chocolate to buy has gotten pretty complicated. Wrapping the eight chocolate bars I bought from my local grocery store (for research purposes only, I assure you) were labels that variously certified them as USDA Organic (4), Fair Trade (4), For Life (2), gluten-free (2), carbon neutral (1), halal (1), non-GMO (1) and vegan (1). Several also had pictures and stories of the heirloom varieties grown, farmers who grow them, the processes by which they were fermented, dried, roasted and made into chocolate. How's a lover to choose?

Shaffer, whose Black Dinah Chocolatiers facility is located near Portland, doesn't buy chocolate that involves slave or child labor, environmental destruction, or unfair pay to farmers. Her confections have won national Good Food awards for being both exceptionally delicious and sourced to support sustainability and social goodness.

"You have to look deeper than the certification labels," Schaffer said, because they don't necessarily tell the whole story. Many cocoa-producing countries opt out of USDA Organic and Fair Trade certifications as their own laws governing that commodity are actually stricter.

"I look for single-source chocolate," Shaffer said. "Not that blends are bad, but if I focus on purchasing chocolate made with beans from a single region, then I can research the production processes in that region and the laws that govern the commodity there." She also looks for chocolate produced in the region where the beans are grown (she mainly chooses chocolate from Venezuela and Peru) because she believes that communities should benefit from the commodity they produce.

Enna Grazier, a cocoa bean-to-chocolate bar maker based in Exeter, New Hampshire, has similar sourcing ideals, but adds one more: cacao genetic biodiversity. Cacao trees, like coffee trees, provide shade cover for a host of species—plant, insect, and animal—in the hot climates in which they grow. Having a diverse gene pool represented in cacao groves will help the population of trees and the species that depend upon them cope with changes in the overall environment. Grazier recommends Madecasse chocolate, which is available at Hannaford, Market Basket, and Whole Foods, and is sourced from heirloom cacao beans grown in Madagascar.

"The benefit of a vast cacao gene pool for chocolate lovers is that each type of bean offers a new and different flavor to the chocolate it gets made into," Grazier said. A detail she feels is well worth noticing.

Storing chocolate

Keep it wrapped tightly, in a dark place with low humidity and an optimal temperature of 65°. Dark chocolate keeps for a year but milk chocolate lasts only six months.

Triple chocolate meringue pie

This recipe is based on one Kate Shaffer of Black Dinah Chocolatiers developed for her book Desserted: Recipes and Tales from an Island Chocolatier. *She's always used sustainable chocolate, but I've woven in several other greener choices into the ingredient list and instructions.*

Makes 1 (9-inch) pie

Crust:

- 1 single piecrust dough
- 2 ounces milk chocolate, chopped and melted

Filling:

- 1/2 cup raw sugar
- 1/4 cup cornstarch
- 1/2 teaspoon kosher salt
- 4 egg yolks
- 3 cups milk
- 5 ounces bittersweet chocolate, chopped and melted
- 2 ounces unsweetened chocolate, chopped and melted
- 2 tablespoons unsalted butter
- 1 teaspoon vanilla extract

Meringue:

- 4 room-temperature egg whites
- 1/2 cup raw sugar, pulsed in a food processor to the consistency of superfine sugar

Preheat oven to 425°.

Roll out dough. Fit it into a 9-inch pie shell. Use a fork to dock holes into crust. Line crust with a piece of parchment paper. Fill lined pie shell with dried beans or pie weights. Bake for 12 minutes. Remove parchment and pie weights, and finish baking crust until bottom is golden and set (3 to 5 minutes). Take crust out of oven and reduce heat to 300°.

Cool crust to room temperature. Spread melted chocolate over the bottom. Let chocolate settle into docking holes to avoid a soggy crust.

Whisk sugar, cornstarch, salt, and egg yolks in a medium-size saucepan. Whisk milk into egg mixture and place the pan over medium heat. Cook, stirring constantly, until mixture comes to a boil. Simmer 1 minute, and remove from heat. Press hot pudding through a fine-mesh sieve into a heat-proof bowl and stir in chocolates, butter, and vanilla. Mix until pudding is smooth. Cool slightly.

Place the egg whites in the bowl of a stand mixer and beat with whisk attachment until they hold soft peaks. While the mixer is running, gradually add superfine raw sugar. Beat until the peaks are stiff and glossy, but not dry or grainy.

Pour warm pudding into prepared crust, leveling it off with an offset icing spatula for best results. Spread the meringue over entire surface of the pie so that it makes contact with the crust around the edges. Place the pie on a sheet pan and slide it into the oven to bake until the meringue is golden and cooked through (20 to 30 minutes). Remove the pie from the oven and cool. Chill the pie for 6 to 8 hours before serving.

MADECASSE
MADAGASCAR CHOCOLATE
70% COCOA
BEAN TO BAR IN AFRICA
ALTER ECO
60%
DARK
ALMOND
NEWMAN'S OWN ORGANICS
70%
SUPER DARK CHOCOLATE
ALMOND

Chili cinnamon chocolate soufflés

I first tasted rustic stone-ground chocolate in Cambridge, Massachusetts. It was made by a Somerville-based company called Taza Chocolate that was on the cutting edge of the ethical cacao sourcing movement. I couldn't decide if I liked the chipotle chili or the cinnamon flavored chocolate at the time. Still can't actually, which is how I arrived at the flavor combination for these soufflés.

Serves 8

Softened butter for coating ramekins

Organic granulated sugar

3/4 cup milk

1 dried chipotle chili pepper

2 tablespoons unsweetened cocoa powder

1 teaspoon pure vanilla extract or paste

1/2 teaspoon ground cinnamon, more for dusting

1/4 teaspoon kosher salt

3 egg yolks, room temperature

2 tablespoons flour mixed with 2 tablespoons cold coffee

3/4 cup finely chopped dark chocolate (preferably stone ground)

6 egg whites, room temperature

Confectioners' sugar, for dusting

Preheat oven to 350°. Coat insides of 8, 6-ounce ramekins with softened butter. Toss a little sugar around the insides of each one, pouring out the excess.

Combine milk, chili pepper, cocoa powder, vanilla, cinnamon, and salt in a small saucepan and bring the mixture to a simmer over medium-high heat. Turn off heat and steep for 30 minutes. Strain and rewarm mixture over low heat.

Whisk yolks and 1/4 cup sugar in a medium bowl until the sugar is evenly distributed.

Slowly (so you don't end up with scrambled eggs) whisk 1/2 cup of the simmering milk mixture into the yolk mixture. This is called tempering. Pour the tempered yolk mixture back into the pot. Whisk over medium heat for one minute. Add flour/coffee mixture, and whisk until thickened (30 to 60 seconds). Remove pan from heat and add chocolate chips, stirring just enough so that the sauce covers the chips to melt them.

Whip egg whites with an electric mixer on high speed. Once they are frothy, drizzle in 1/2 cup sugar while continuing to whip them. Continue whipping egg whites until they hold their peaks.

Transfer the chocolate mixture to a large bowl. Add whipped whites, one-third at a time, folding slowly and gently until they are fully incorporated. Spoon mixture into prepared ramekins, filling them about 3/4 full.

Bake for 30 minutes. Dust with confectioners' sugar and ground cinnamon and serve immediately.

Christine

Savor every last bite of your apples and lemons

It's not like I'm comparing apples and lemons. Well, yes, I am. In my kitchen, these two disparate fruits are commonplace while not being from a common place.

Local apples abound in Maine. They come from commercial orchards, others from organic ones, still more from heritage orchards, and a random few from apple trees in friends' backyards. In spite of warming temperatures, no lemons (or any citrus at all) grow here. Whether my fruit is locally abundant or had to travel cross-country, I still try to use every last scrap.

I thought my great-grandmother Mabel was a culinary genius when I was seven because she could remove the peel from any apple with a paring knife in a single, spiraling strip. She'd challenge any of us underfoot to eat the peels without breaking them in a fashion that required putting our hands behind our backs and having the long helixes stretch from our mouths to our knees. I've since found a few more ways to use all of the apple bits.

The cores can be turned into apple cider vinegar. This process requires a quart mason jar packed tightly with cores (15 to 20 depending on the size of the apples) and 3 tablespoons of raw sugar dissolved in 2 cups of filtered water (not tap water treated with chlorine as that will stop the fermentation process). Cover the jar with several layers of cheesecloth secured with the jar's ring and place it in a warm corner for a week, giving it a daily stir. Strain the liquid into a clean jar. Cover again with cheesecloth and the jar's ring, and put it in a cool cabinet to ferment for a month.

My simplest solution for peels is not to peel any apple going into applesauce. Simmer apples skin-on and push them through a food mill when they're soft to give the sauce a beautifully rosy hue. If you do peel your apples, use the peels for the sauce of Veiled Country Lass (150), flavor and dry the peels in a low oven for a snack (Cinnamon-and-Spice Apple Peel Crisps, 151) or steep the peels from 1½ pounds of apples in a 750-ml bottle of bourbon with a cinnamon stick and a few cloves for three days at room temperature for a tasty treat of another kind.

For the citrus, I use the colorful zest and the tangy juice of every fruit I buy.

I heartily thank the Canadian housewife who grabbed her husband's microplane rasp from the workshop and repurposed it as a less bloody-knuckle alternate to the box grater for taking the zest from any citrus fruit. But my favorite zesting tool is called, well, a zester. It's a short-handled tool with a stainless steel top that resembles a stubby hand. The finger tips in this descriptive analogy are round

Apple agradolce

This sweet and sour syrup glazes pork, flavors seltzer and anchors salad dressings. Simmer 10 apple cores, 1 cup of vinegar, ⅔ cup each raw sugar and water, and 3 sprigs of fresh thyme until the liquid reduces to one cup. Strain, cool, and store in the refrigerator.

Spice up simple syrup

The syrup left over from making candied peel already has a citrus taste. Adding rosemary (or thyme or a whole hot chili) to the jar in which it is stored, makes the flavor more complex.

blades. You drag those blades along the outside of the lemon (or any other citrus fruit on hand) for long, curly pieces of zest that can be candied.

Candied lemon peel (Lavendar Lemon Posset with Candied Lemon Peel, 152) is a satisfying late afternoon nibble and can decoratively elevate winter desserts. You can use the syrup from the candying process as a glaze for a pound cake or a sweetener for a lemony cocktail.

Without its protective coating, naked citrus dries out quickly. So immediately following the zesting process, I juice lemons, limes, oranges or grapefruits as the case may be, into ice cube trays and freeze cubes for fish dishes like Crispy Whole Fish with Spicy Soy Dipping Sauce (115). I stuff the spent citrus carcasses into a jar of vinegar with a few herbs. After a couple of weeks under my kitchen sink, I've got an all-purpose detergent to help clean it and any other surface in the kitchen.

Veiled country lass, page 150

Veiled country lass

This recipe is an adaptation of one by Graham Kerr, an English cooking personality whose show The Galloping Gourmet *aired on PBS in the 1960s. My English mother-in-law was a fan and served this dessert one of the first times I ate at her table. I was a lass from the country, although I did not wear a veil in her presence until my wedding. This recipe calls for white bread crumbs, but the dessert has its roots in Scandinavia, where it's called Peasant Girls in the Mist and uses dark rye bread crumbs. Maine farmer and cookbook writer Margaret Hathaway of Ten Apple Farm makes a version with challah, cocoa, and apple brandy. So there is a proven track record for its being adapted to taste.*

Serves 8

4 tablespoons unsalted butter, plus more to prepare the cake pan

¼ cup raw sugar

7 cups fresh white breadcrumbs

⅛ teaspoon ground cinnamon

2 cups applesauce

1 cup raspberry jam, plus 2 to 3 tablespoons for decorating

2 cups heavy cream

Preheat oven to 350°. Butter bottom and sides of a 7-inch springform pan.

Melt butter over medium-high heat in a large skillet. Add sugar and stir until melted (2 minutes). Add breadcrumbs and sauté, stirring periodically, until they are golden and crisp (10 to 12 minutes). Stir in cinnamon.

Press a scant 2 cups of the crumb mixture into the bottom of the prepared cake pan. Spread 1 cup of applesauce on top of the crumbs and ½ cup of jam on top of the applesauce. Repeat the layering process—breadcrumbs, applesauce, and jam—one more time. End by spreading 1½ cups of crumbs as the top layer. Reserve the remaining ½ cup of seasoned crumbs for decoration.

Bake for 20 minutes. Remove cake from the oven and allow it to cool completely in the pan. Refrigerate for at least 2 hours. Run a knife around the inside circumference of the pan before trying to release the cake.

Whip cream to stiff peaks and slather it on the cooled cake. Decorate with remaining breadcrumbs and extra jam. Keep chilled for up to 3 hours before serving.

Cinnamon-and-spice apple peel crisps

This recipe takes the peels from apples used in a pie and turns them into a crunchy snack. The time in the oven required to make them crispy will depend on how much apple flesh comes off with the peels when you're prepping them. My great-grandmother Mabel used a paring knife, but there's less waste using a vegetable peeler.

Makes 2 loosely packed cups

3 tablespoons sugar

1/2 teaspoon kosher salt

1/2 teaspoon cinnamon

1/4 teaspoon ground ginger

1/8 teaspoon cayenne pepper

Peels from 6 to 8 large apples (about 4 cups loosely packed)

Preheat oven to 200°. Line 2 baking sheets with silicone mats.

Combine sugar, salt, cinnamon, ginger, and cayenne in a large bowl. Add peels. Toss to coat. The peels will break into manageable sizes during the coating process. Divide peels between the prepared baking sheets, spreading them out so that none are touching. Bake for 2 to 2½ hours, rotating sheets every 30 minutes, until the edges of the peels curl in on each other and the skins darken to a light brown. Cool completely. Store in an airtight container for 2 to 3 days.

Lavender lemon posset with candied lemon peel

This is a recipe based on one introduced to me by my virtual-world friend Liz Larkin of Pound Ridge, New York. It's ironic that we share a real-world connection to High Lawn Farm in Lee, Massachusetts. I grew up on the milk of the Jersey cows on that farm, and her relatives delivered it around the county. The cream from Jersey cows makes this simple custard simply decadent.

Serves 8

Candied zest:

- 4 lemons
- 1¼ cups organic granulated sugar

Pudding:

- 2 cups heavy cream
- ½ cup honey
- 2 teaspoons dried culinary lavender
- 5 tablespoons lemon juice

To make the zest, use either a citrus zesting tool or a vegetable peeler to remove the peel from the fruit in long pieces, getting as little of the pith as possible. If you used a peeler, take a sharp knife and slice the peel into thin strips. Place julienned zest in a small bowl; cover with boiling water. Let stand 30 minutes, then drain.

Place 1 cup sugar and 1 cup water in a saucepan over medium-high heat. Stir until the sugar has dissolved. Add zest. Reduce heat to medium. Simmer zest until it is slightly opaque (12 to 15 minutes).

Drain zest, reserving syrup for other uses. Allow zest to sit in strainer for 30 minutes to dry slightly. Place ¼ cup sugar in a large bowl. Add drained zest and toss. Shake off excess sugar and place candied zest on a dry towel. After it has dried for 2 hours, transfer zest to an airtight container and store at room temperature for up to 2 weeks.

Note: Other citrus zest (limes, Meyer lemons, oranges, or blood oranges) can be candied in this manner as well.

To make the pudding, heat cream and honey in a medium saucepan over medium heat, stirring constantly, until small bubbles appear on the edges. Do not let it boil. Remove from heat, stir in lavender and steep for 30 minutes.

Strain lavender from sweetened cream and return cream to medium heat to simmer for 5 minutes. Remove pan from heat and stir in lemon juice. Cool mixture for 15 minutes. Divide evenly among 8 small ramekins. Refrigerate at least 2 hours, until set.

Garnish with a pinch of candied zest.

Christine

Local sugar substitutes sweeten things up

If it's your sweetie's birthday, your wedding anniversary, or Valentine's Day skip the roses. Chances are they were shipped in from South America, are covered in pesticides, and carry a hefty carbon footprint. Perhaps a homemade gift made with local maple syrup or honey might be a more sustainable option.

If given to your beloved in the form of heart-shaped candies, poured over breakfast-in-bed pancakes (Multi-grain Homemade Pancake Mix, 23) or used in homemade baked goods (Maple Pecan Cream Tart, 157), these local sweeteners can also be very romantic.

Maine maple syrup and value-added products like granulated maple sugar and maple butter or cream (syrup that has been reduced and whipped) are easily found online at sugarhouse sites or in many a brick-and-mortar local food shop.

Even if your recipe isn't written with maple syrup or honey as an ingredient, you can use them in place of other sweeteners. But when making those substitutions, you need to keep a few facts in mind.

All maple syrup bottled in America is sold as U.S. Grade A quality, but it is further classified by color and flavor as golden (delicate flavor), amber (rich flavor), amber dark (robust flavor) and very dark (strong flavor). View the variation as a challenge, not an obstacle.

Maple syrup and honey are both sweeter than white sugar. If a recipe calls for 1 cup of granulated white sugar, use ¾ cup of maple syrup or honey and decrease the other liquid in the recipe by 2 tablespoons. The Maine Maple Producers Association website also recommends adding ¼ to ½ teaspoon of baking soda to any baking recipes into which you are fitting maple syrup to help cakes or cookies rise, unless the recipe already calls for buttermilk, sour milk, or sour cream, which are already acidic. It's also a good idea to reduce the baking time and temperature slightly to prevent burning.

You can swap any maple syrup in equal measure when a recipe calls for other natural liquid sweeteners like honey or agave and vice versa. But because corn syrup is often employed for its high levels of invert sugars (chemically split sugars that help ward off crystallization), you can't substitute maple syrup for it in complicated confections or high-heat candies, I am afraid, so use recipes that are written especially for them (Salted Pumpkin Caramels, 160).

Granulated maple sugar can be substituted one-for-one for granulated white sugar. It adds the most intense maple flavor to baked recipes because the natural water content of maple syrup is removed. It's particularly good for producing crispy baked goods (Maple Walnut Shortbread Crisps, 156).

Raw sugar—technically called turbinado sugar—come, from sugarcane juice as does the majority of refined white sugar. The main difference is that with refined sugar, the cane juice is boiled three times to remove all of its natural molasses ,whereas to make raw sugar, it is only boiled once to remove impurities. It takes less energy to produce raw sugar. Also, since raw sugar has a richer taste due to much of the molasses still being in the mix, I use less of it in my recipes (Triple Chocolate

Reversing crystallization

If the honey in your jar has gone lumpy, simply set the jar in a bowl of 100° water until it smooths out. Remove it from the water and cool as quickly as possible.

Meringue Pie, 144).

To elevate the flavor of local, liquid sweeteners, use complementary ingredients. Maple's BFFs are bourbon (Maple Bourbon Apple Vinaigrette, 174), butter (Maple Chipotle Cilantro Butter, 169), celery (Date Night Fennel and Celery Salad, 44), walnuts (Banana Walnut Waffles, 24), and rum (Spiced Maple Custard Pie, 159). For honey lovers, those flavor boosters include cream (Honeyed Little Boy's Pudding, 162), lemon (Lavender Lemon Posset, 152), mustard (Honey Curried Chicken, 107), orange (Honey Orange Blossom Dressing, 174), and vanilla (Honey, Vanilla, and Black Pepper Cantaloupe Seeds, 185).

Adding those to whatever you decide to mix up for your sweetheart can only help sustain his or her devotion to local sweeteners—and to you.

ock cherry pie filling,
age 163

Maple walnut shortbread crisps

My husband's favorite ice cream is maple walnut. He adores shortbread. I developed this recipe for him. If you can't find maple butter/cream, but still want to make a glaze for these cookies, combine 2 tablespoons each of maple syrup and confectioners' sugar, 1 tablespoon melted butter, and a pinch of sea salt.

Makes 1 dozen cookies

1 1/4 cups white whole wheat flour

1/2 teaspoon kosher salt

6 tablespoons unsalted butter, at room temperature

1/3 cup granulated maple sugar, plus 1 tablespoon for sprinkling

1/4 cup maple syrup

1/4 cup finely chopped walnuts

1/4 cup maple butter/cream (for optional glaze)

Whisk flour and salt in a small bowl. Use an electric mixer to cream butter and 1/3 cup granulated maple sugar in a larger bowl. Slowly beat in maple syrup. Add flour and mix until just combined. Stir in walnuts. Wrap dough in plastic and refrigerate for 30 minutes.

Preheat oven to 325°.

Roll the dough on a silicone mat to 1/4-inch thickness and cut it into shapes. Leave the cookies in place, by simply pulling excess dough away from the cutouts. You can keep the cookies pretty close together because this dough will not spread in the oven. (I cook the scraps on a separate baking sheet for a cook's treat or mix them into vanilla ice cream for a maple walnut cookie dough effect.)

Transfer the mat with cookies to a baking sheet. Sprinkle cookies with remaining 1 tablespoon of granulated maple sugar and bake until edges are light brown but cookies are still soft (12 to 15 minutes).

Remove from oven and cool on baking sheet for 5 minutes until cookies harden a bit. Transfer to a wire rack to cool completely.

Warm maple butter/cream slightly and drizzle it over (or use it to decorate) cooled cookies.

Maple pecan cream tart

The light and airy crust on this tart is what it's all about. It works well with almost any kind of tree nut.

Makes one 8 by 11-inch rectangular tart

Butter

½ cup raw sugar, pulsed in a processor to get it to a fine grain

½ cup granulated maple sugar

3 egg whites, room temperature

⅛ teaspoon salt

½ cup maple syrup

¾ cup chopped pecans, toasted

¾ cup unsalted soda crackers, crushed

1 teaspoon baking powder

16 pecan halves

1 cup heavy whipping cream

Preheat oven to 350°. Butter bottom and sides of an 8 by 11-inch rectangular tart pan. A large round one will work, too. Regardless of the pan's shape, it's best that it have a removable bottom.

Combine the sugars in a small bowl. Combine egg whites and salt in a large mixing bowl and beat them with an electric mixer at high speed until they've formed soft peaks. Keep whipping as you slowly add sugars, 2 tablespoons at a time until it is incorporated and you've got glossy peaks.

Slowly mix in 2 tablespoons maple syrup. Fold in chopped pecans, crackers and baking powder. Spread the mixture into the prepared tart pan, taking care to make the sides high, so that there is a good indentation in the middle to (eventually) hold maple whipped cream.

Bake the shell until meringue is golden but not brown (25 to 35 minutes). Remove from oven and cool completely. Refrigerate shell at least 2 hours, preferably overnight.

Meanwhile, pour ¼ cup maple syrup in a nonstick skillet and add pecan halves, coating them with syrup. Cook over medium-high heat, letting the syrup bubble around nuts. When syrup is caramelized and sticky and nuts are coated, they are sufficiently candied. Lift nuts out of the pan and cool them on a silicone mat.

When you are ready to serve the tart, whip cream to soft peaks. Add 2 tablespoons of maple syrup and whip cream a bit more. Spread cream throughout meringue cavity. Top with candied pecans and serve. You can store the filled tart in the refrigerator for several hours.

Spiced maple custard pie

Former Maine Pie Line shop owner, Brianna Warner, gave me her recipe for maple nutmeg custard pie just before she left the pastry business in 2014. With this adaptation, I've warmed up the custard with black pepper, cinnamon, and ginger, deepened the maple flavor with granulated maple sugar, and spiced up the crust via cinnamon graham crackers.

Serves 8

1½ cups heavy cream

½ cup maple syrup

2 cinnamon sticks, broken in pieces

10 black peppercorns, cracked

¼ teaspoon freshly grated nutmeg, more for garnish

1 pinch kosher salt

4 (¼-inch) slices of candied ginger

1½ cups finely ground cinnamon graham crackers (20 squares)

1 tablespoon sugar

5 tablespoons butter, melted

5 egg yolks, lightly beaten

¼ cup granulated maple sugar

1 tablespoon spiced rum (optional)

Whipped cream for serving

Combine cream, maple syrup, cinnamon, peppercorns, nutmeg, and salt in a saucepan and place it over medium-high heat. When cream begins to simmer, remove it from the heat. Drop candied ginger slices into hot cream. Allow mixture to steep while crust bakes and cools, about 45 minutes.

Preheat oven to 375°.

To make the crust, combine cracker crumbs, sugar, and butter in a bowl until evenly moistened. Press mixture into the bottom and up the sides of a 9-inch pie plate. Bake crust until it is set and slightly golden brown around its edges (10 to 12 minutes). Cool completely on wire rack.

To make the filling, whisk egg yolks and granulated maple sugar in a medium bowl. Set aside.

Strain steeped cream to remove spices. Reheat cream and very slowly whisk it into egg mixture. Once the cream is fully incorporated into eggs, pour mixture back into the pan and place it over medium heat. Stir continuously (or eggs may scramble) until mixture thickens enough to coat the back of a spoon (6 to 8 minutes). If they did scramble in spite of your careful attention, pour custard through a fine-meshed sieve to strain out the eggy bits. Stir in rum, if using.

Pour filling into cooled crust. Chill pie for at least 2 hours before serving heaped with whipped cream.

Salted pumpkin caramels

A less sustainable version of this recipe won me accolades as the 2010 Best Halloween Treat on the curated food website, Food52.com. This one nixes the white sugar and corn syrup and still seems to be a winner.

Makes 64 caramels

⅔ cup unsalted pepitas (hulled pumpkin seeds)

1½ cups heavy cream

⅔ cup pumpkin puree

1½ teaspoons pumpkin pie spice

2 cups organic granulated sugar

1 cup maple syrup

4 tablespoons unsalted butter, cut in chunks

1 teaspoon lemon juice

¾ teaspoon Maine sea salt

Toast the pepitas in a dry skillet over medium heat until they start to pop (1 to 2 minutes). Remove pan from heat. Line bottom and sides of an 8-inch square pan with parchment. Butter the parchment on the sides of the pan. Spread toasted pepitas evenly around prepared pan.

Combine the cream, pumpkin puree, and pumpkin pie spice in a small saucepan and warm over low heat. Set aside.

In a heavy-bottomed pan, at least 4 inches deep, combine sugar, syrup, and ¼ cup of water. Place pan over medium-high heat. Stir mixture until sugar is dissolved. Dip a heat-safe pastry brush in warm water and brush any sugar granules off the sides of the pan to prevent them from crystallizing. Attach a candy thermometer to the side of the pan. Boil until the syrup reaches 250°. Then, very carefully, stir in the cream-and-pumpkin mixture.

Over medium heat, bring the combined mixture back to 245°. This can take a while—as much as 30 minutes—but don't leave the kitchen. Watch it carefully and stir the mixture more frequently once it reaches 230° to keep it from burning.

As soon as it reaches 245°, pull it off the heat and whisk in butter and lemon juice until both are fully incorporated. Pour caramel into prepared pan. Cool 30 minutes, then sprinkle with salt. Let the caramel fully set (at least 4 hours) before using a hot knife to cut them into 1-inch squares. Wrap them individually in parchment or waxed paper. Caramels will keep at room temperature for a week.

Chewy, spicy, birch syrup lumberjack cookies

Birch syrup is maple syrup's sassier cousin. But the former adds an interesting twist to these spicy chewy cookies that people won't place until you tell them. Think of it as money well spent for teatime conversation. Filling your own jars with whole spices reduces unnecessary packaging. Grinding them just before mixing them into the batter provides the best flavor.

Makes 24 cookies

2¼ cups all-purpose flour

2 teaspoons baking soda

2 teaspoons ground ginger

1 teaspoon ground cinnamon

½ teaspoon mustard powder

½ teaspoon allspice

½ teaspoon kosher salt

¼ teaspoon black pepper

¾ cup unsalted butter (1½ sticks), room temperature

1 cup packed light brown sugar

1 large egg

½ cup birch syrup (or molasses)

⅓ cup finely diced candied ginger (optional)

Raw sugar for rolling

Preheat oven to 375°. Line two large baking sheets with silicone mats.

Whisk flour, baking soda, ground ginger, cinnamon, mustard powder, allspice, salt, and black pepper.

Beat butter and sugar together in bowl of stand mixer until light and fluffy (2 to 3 minutes). Add egg and birch syrup. Mix well. Stir in dry ingredients. Stir in candied ginger, if using. Refrigerate dough for 30 minutes.

Roll dough into 1½-inch balls and then roll them in raw sugar. Arrange on baking sheets and gently flatten them with the bottom of a flat glass. Bake until set and crinkled on top (10 to 12 minutes).

Cool cookies on a baking sheet for 2 minutes and transfer them to a rack to cool completely.

Honeyed little boy's pudding

Serves 4 generously

6 tablespoons butter, melted

3/4 cup short grain rice

1/3 cup honey

4 cups of whole milk

1/4 teaspoon ground ginger

1/4 teaspoon kosher salt

Dried or fresh fruit to serve (optional)

This recipe is adapted from one printed in 1846 in Miss Catherine Beecher's Domestic Receipt-Book: Designed as a Supplement to Her Treatise on Domestic Economy *when it was meant to be a dessert served in the nursery. Catherine was by reputation a much better cook than her sister, Harriet Beecher Stowe, whose Brunswick, Maine, home is right down the street from mine. Rice pudding also happens to be my husband's favorite dessert, but he likes it without dried fruit on principle. If you are less principled about your pudding, adding finely chopped dried apricots to the mix before baking would be a nice change.*

Preheat oven to 250°.

Pour melted butter into an oven-safe, 2-quart, shallow baking dish. Add all other ingredients. Stir. Bake until rice is swollen (2 hours). If you prefer a pudding with a thick skin on top, stir 2 to 3 times early during the pudding's time in the oven and then stop stirring. If you want to avoid having a skin, stir early and often. Let sit 10 minutes before serving.

Mock cherry pie filling

Many of the community cookbooks from towns in New Hampshire and Maine held as part of the Esta Kramer Collection of American Cookery at Bowdoin College contain recipes for mock cherry pie filling. I lived for 12 years in central Pennsylvania, where I spent the first two weeks of every July frantically canning sour cherries, so I consider myself an expert, and I was suspicious that this combination could even come close to my dad's favorite pie filling. I was proven wrong.

Makes enough filling for 1 pie

4 cups whole Maine cranberries (fresh or frozen)

2/3 cups golden raisins

1 1/4 cups raw sugar

1 1/2 tablespoons all-purpose flour

1 teaspoon lemon zest

2 tablespoons cherry liqueur (optional)

1/2 cup water

Combine all ingredients in a medium saucepan over medium-high heat. Bring to a simmer, reduce heat, and cook until cranberries pop and mixture thickens slightly (6 to 8 minutes). Cool mixture to room temperature. At this juncture, it's ready to use in a pie or can be stored in the refrigerator for up to a week.

Kale chimichurri sauce, page 17

Finishing touches

Christine

Compound butter is an aging herb's best friend

Fresh herbs make most things taste better. I always have a bunch hanging around, wrapped in a clean towel in my refrigerator's crisper. Whether I've taken the time to cultivate an herb garden of my own (that's only happened once so far) or spent the cash to buy fresh herbs at the market (a more regular occurrence), I'm loath to waste one teeny, tiny, thyme leaf.

But no matter what pains I take to extend the lives of my herbs, eventually they will die wastefully if I don't do something useful with them.

Enter fat. The two best substances for carrying a flavor throughout a dish are alcohol and fat. I tend to take the former straight up. But both butter and olive oil in my kitchen are my best bets for herbs headed to the freezer before they die. Since it's the herbs' oils that give each its distinct flavor and aroma, preserving them in fat helps them to hold their distinctive tastes.

The leaves of green herbs like rosemary, thyme, oregano, parsley, cilantro, and basil can all be frozen with an equal amount of neutral oil in ice cube trays or freezer safe bags. They can then be taken out in chunks and used in soups, sautés, and salad dressings like you would use fresh herbs.

But since I agree with Julia Child's assertions about everything going better with butter, and that even moderation should be taken in moderation, I preserve my aging herbs in good quality, local, unsalted butter. To make a compound butter that will upgrade warm bread, baked fillets of fish, grilled pieces of steak, hot cups of rice, and bowls of steamed vegetables merely by sitting on top of them, you combine ½ cup of softened unsalted butter with 2 tablespoons of minced herbs, spices, cooked and cooled aromatics, and salt.

The finished flavored butter gets formed into a log either using a recycled butter wrapper or a clean piece of parchment paper. It can be stored in the refrigerator for a week or the freezer for up to 2 months. Just slice off a thin disk any time you need a little butter to carry your herbs to the plate.

The nine lives of a butter wrapper:
Compound butter wrapper. Corn on the Cob Butter Conveyor. Pan Greaser. Muffin Liner. Pudding Skin Preventer. Chicken Baster. Baked Fish Liner. Hamburger Patty Separator. Fireplace Fire Starter.

Compound butter combos

All compound butter recipes on pages 168 and 169 use the same method.

Makes 24 servings

Start with one stick (8 tablespoons or 4 ounces) of unsalted, room-temperature butter. Either mash the butter on a cutting board with a fork, cream it in a bowl with a wooden spoon, or beat lightly with an electric mixer.

Add liquids, such as lemon juice or hot sauce, to the butter first. Any cooked ingredients—say sautéed shallots—should be cooked dry and cooled before being added to the butter. Add raw ingredients (minced, grated, or chopped very finely), next. Spices and salts should be added last and used sparingly as the butterfat amplifies their flavor.

Form the compound butter into a log that is about 6 inches long and 1 inch in diameter. Wrap it in either a recycled butter wrapper or a clean piece of parchment. Store in the refrigerator for one week or in the freezer for two months. Slice ¼-inch per serving.

ɔ: Garlic greens and lemon butter, page 168
ddle: Maple Chipotle cilantro butter, page 169
ttom: Shallot, mushroom thyme butter, 169

Garlic greens and lemon butter

Use green garlic in May, garlic scapes in June, and garlic chives thereafter. This butter can be used to make garlic bread or stuffed under chicken skin prior to roasting. And it makes a killer topping for grilled oysters.

1 teaspoon lemon juice

1 tablespoon plus 1 teaspoon minced garlic greens

½ teaspoon lemon zest

½ teaspoon sea salt

Chive horseradish butter

Excellent on beef steak, meaty fish fillets, baked potatoes, and roasted beets. It's also wonderful stirred into apple sauce.

1½ teaspoons prepared horseradish

3 teaspoons minced fresh chives

1 teaspoon lemon zest

½ teaspoon celery salt

Maple chipotle cilantro butter

Great for salmon, pork, corn on the cob, and sweet potatoes

1 teaspoon maple syrup

1 teaspoon minced chipotle in adobo sauce

1 tablespoon minced cilantro

½ teaspoon orange zest

½ teaspoon kosher salt

Shallot mushroom thyme butter

Elegant finishing touch for steamed asparagus, warm whole wheat berries or barley side dishes, and scrambled eggs.

1 tablespoon minced shallot, sautéed and cooled

1½ teaspoons dried mushroom powder

1 teaspoon minced thyme leaves

½ teaspoon sea salt

Christine

DIY salad dressing skips the chemicals

When I throw a dinner party, I always serve a cheese course with a lightly dressed salad between the entrée and dessert. It's little bother because I set out both on the counter before my guests arrive. The cheese settles to room temperature as dinner progresses while a simple vinaigrette sits blended in the bottom of a bowl under naked greens until it's time to be tossed.

Compare the vinegar, mustard, minced shallot, salt, pepper, and oil used to make classic French vinaigrette with the difficult-to-pronounce ingredient list on a bottle of Hidden Valley Ranch. Still, I buy the latter occasionally because I've never successfully replicated it in my own kitchen.

To counterbalance my contribution to the $2 billion salad dressing market, I make sure the vast majority of my hot and cold salads are dolled up with combinations of ingredients I already have on hand, stored in reusable glass jars for up to a week in the fridge, are devoid of highly processed oils and chemicals, and mixed by hand.

Choosing the right dressing for any salad is a science, according to J. Kenji Lopez-Alt in his 958-page opus, *The Food Lab: Better Home Cooking Through Science*. He takes sixty of those pages to explain the three families of dressings and how to pair them.

Vinaigrettes (forced mixtures of three parts oil, one part acid, and ⅓ part emulsifying agent like mustard or honey that help keep the acid suspended in the oil like my Maple Bourbon Apple Vinaigrette, 174) are the best bet for simple salads, whether they comprise fresh greens, crunchy colorful slaws (Sweet and Sour Slaw Dressing, 172), or blanched green vegetables. Lopez-Alt explains that going through the trouble to slowly whisk the oil into the vinegar drop by drop to create an emulsion keeps the oil from making the greens soggy.

Mayonnaise-based dressings begin with a raw egg-yolk emulsion and are thicker, creamier and more stable. They require hardier elements in the salad mix, think classic American potato or trendy kale Caesar.

Dairy-based dressings start with a bacterially thickened product like sour cream or buttermilk to which all the other flavors get added. Lopez-Alt saves these for either the classic blue cheese iceberg wedge (Bacon, Buttermilk, and Blue Cheese Dressing, 172), Greek chopped salads where all the disparate parts get a light coating of the stuff, or for dipping, like with ranch, for which he does offer up a recipe. It's good, but it's no Hidden Valley.

Balancing act
If your dressing is too salty, add something sweet. If it's too sour, add something creamy. If it's too sweet, add something meaty (anchovies!)

Sweet and sour slaw dressing, page 172

Sweet and sour slaw dressing

Makes about 1½ cups

1 cup orange juice

Zest of 1 lime

¼ cup lime juice

¼ cup finely chopped cilantro, plus 2 tablespoons for garnish

2 tablespoons finely chopped mint

1 tablespoon honey

1 tablespoon olive oil

2 teaspoon toasted sesame oil

1 teaspoon sea salt

I use this low-fat dressing mainly on slaws made of whatever vegetables I can shred from the crisper drawer in the refrigerator. It goes well with either Asian or Latin foods, and can serve as a cleansing side for rich dishes like roasted duck or pulled pork.

In a glass jar, combine orange juice, lime zest and juice, herbs, honey, oils, and salt. Give it a good shake to combine. Store in the refrigerator for up to 2 weeks.

Bacon, buttermilk, and blue cheese dressing

Makes 2 cups

¾ cup crumbled blue cheese

⅔ cup prepared mayonnaise (full fat is best)

½ cup buttermilk

¼ cup room temperature bacon fat

1 tablespoon red wine vinegar

2 garlic cloves, roughly chopped

½ to 1 teaspoon hot sauce

Freshly ground black pepper

When I either make or buy good, sustainable bacon I notice how crystal clear the grease left in the pan is. So I strain it into a glass bowl that I cover and refrigerate. I lie in wait until a good blue cheese makes its way into my kitchen, and then I make this decadent dressing that has more calories than hot fudge and is worth the dietary tradeoff for sure!

Place all ingredients except freshly ground black pepper in the bowl of a food processor. Pulse until mixture is well blended and has only small chunks in it. Season with pepper to taste. Store in a glass container in the refrigerator for up to a week.

Bacon, buttermilk, and blue cheese dressing, page 172

Honey orange blossom dressing

Makes a generous cup

½ cup olive oil

¼ cup honey

¼ cup lemon juice (Meyer Lemons if you can get them)

4 teaspoons sherry vinegar

2 teaspoons orange blossom water

1 teaspoon kosher salt

½ teaspoon cracked black pepper

I developed this dressing to go with the Golden and Ruby Beets with Goat Cheese, Pistachios, and Microgreens (70) but have used it to marinate chicken, to flavor roasted carrots, and as a warm dressing for chickpea, red onion, and arugula salads.

In a pint jar with a lid, combine oil, honey, lemon juice, vinegar, orange blossom water, salt, and pepper. Put the cover on and give it a good shake until the honey is completely dissolved. Store in the refrigerator for up to a week.

Maple bourbon apple vinaigrette

Makes a scant cup

2 tablespoons minced shallot

¼ cup apple cider vinegar

2 tablespoons maple syrup

1 tablespoon bourbon

1 teaspoon Dijon mustard

1 teaspoon kosher salt

½ cup neutral oil

This is a classic French-style vinaigrette with an American maple bourbon twist. This dressing goes best with a hearty salad that also has bacon and spinach in the mix. I use a vinegar easily made from apple cores left over from a pie I make in the fall (Read "Savor Every Last Bite of Your Apples and Lemons Apples and Lemons," 148), but any apple cider vinegar will work.

Combine vinegar and shallots in a bowl. Let sit 15 minutes. Stir maple syrup, bourbon, mustard and salt into the bowl. While continuing to whisk the mixture with a metal bulb whisk, very slowly add the oil drop by drop. The dressing will begin to emulsify—become thicker as the oil gets suspended in the vinegar mixture—and you can start to add the oil in a steady stream, whisking all the while. Store in an airtight jar for up to a week.

Tomato and basil flower vinaigrette

I only make this when it's high season for tomatoes. It packs an extra tomato-y punch in my Day-Old Bread and Mozzarella Salad (54). Since most basil leaves get either served with the tomatoes in caprese salads or pressed into service as the anchor to a genovese pesto, I use the plants' stems and its bolting flowers—which carry as much flavor as its leaves—as the basis for this tasty condiment.

Makes 1½ cups

2 large, ripe beefsteak tomatoes

2 teaspoons grated garlic

3 tablespoons minced basil flowers

3 tablespoons very finely minced basil stems

2 tablespoons red wine vinegar

¼ cup olive oil

Kosher salt and pepper

Cut the tomatoes in half. Squeeze their seeds and gel into a small bowl. Set aside.

Grate cut sides of tomatoes on the large holes of a boxed grater into a large bowl, compost the skins. Place reserved seeds and their gel (there is tons of flavor in that gel!) into a fine-mesh strainer over the bowl. Use a rubber spatula to push the gel through the sieve, compost the seeds.

Stir garlic, basil flowers and stems, and vinegar into grated tomato mixture. Whisk in olive oil. Add salt and pepper to taste. Store in the refrigerator for up to a week.

Christine

When making a batch of pesto, think ratios, not recipes

Most people think of pesto as the classic Genovese combination of basil, pine nuts, garlic, olive oil, and grated cheese pounded to a paste with a mortar and pestle. But in truth, it's just a means by which you can preserve fresh herbs with a variety of other ingredients into a mixture that can be tossed with everything from agnolotti to ziti and slathered on anything from crusty bread to grilled crustaceans.

More sustainable than a pesto recipe is a ratio. Ratios are generally expressed with the largest quantity first and move on down the line. Recipe ingredient lists are generally written in the order in which they are used in the recipe first, and according to descending quantities second. So this ratio recipes pulls a bit from both structures and goes something like this: 3 cups; to 1 cup; to ⅓ cup; to 1 garlic clove; to ½ cup; to ½ cup; to taste.

The first component is always going to be the herbs (basil, cilantro, mint, oregano, parsley, thyme) and greens (arugula, beet, chard, kale, mustard, spinach) in some combination. You'll need 3 loosely packed cups altogether of these.

Many pestos contain a secondary flavor component, mainly a sweeter one like corn, peas, roasted red peppers or sun-dried tomatoes. I hold these elements to 1 cup to keep the fresh herbs in the starring role.

The third element is nuts. Pignoli (the Italian word for pine nuts) are traditional, but expensive because it's a pretty arduous process to take the seeds from the pinecone and then shell them. While no nut is wholly sustainable given their water requirements, walnuts, pistachios, almonds, and pecans as well as some seeds like pepitas and sunflowers work well in pesto, too. You'll need ⅓ cup. Toasting releases their oils, thereby boosting the flavor for a relatively small volume.

The pungency of pesto comes from the garlic, but how strong your clove is will vary. I start with 1 large one and move up as I need to, but I rarely do.

Mash these ingredients together using a mortar and pestle if you've got a big one, or a food processor if you don't, before processing ½ cup oil—traditionally olive oil if your herbs are strong but you can use more neutral ones if your herbs are more timid. Taste the pesto at this juncture, adding lemon zest and juice to lighten its taste if necessary and a pinch of cayenne if it needs heat.

Only add the cheese, ½ cup of a grated hard one, if you are going to put the pesto in the refrigerator and use it up within a few days. If you plan to freeze it, and you can do so for up to six months, it's best to do so without the cheese. Ice cube trays are great for this job. Add 1 tablespoon of cheese to every cube of thawed pesto when you use it, whenever that may be.

Pesto

To thin out pesto for use with pasta, place pesto in a large bowl with ¼ cup of pasta cooking water. Drain pasta and toss it with the watered down pesto, which will become creamier due to the starch in the water.

Corn cilantro pesto

I've made this as many times in my Mexican molcajete (mortar) and tejolete (pestle) as I've made it my food processor. This is a perfect condiment for Fish Tacos (112). Toss the extra pesto with raw zucchini ribbons, cooked fettucine and ¼ cup of pasta water for a second meal.

Makes 2 cups including
+ Plan-over for pasta dish

2 cups loosely packed spinach leaves

1 cup loosely packed cilantro leaves

1 cup fresh corn kernels

⅓ cup toasted pepitas

1 garlic clove

½ cup neutral oil

1 teaspoon lime zest

1 teaspoon lime juice

Kosher salt

Cayenne pepper

½ cup finely grated hard cheese (Dry Jack or Pecorino works)

Combine spinach, cilantro, corn, pepitas, and garlic in the bowl of a food processor. Pulse until the mixture is a fine paste. With the machine running, slowly pour in oil until it is fully incorporated. Stir in lime zest and juice. Add salt and cayenne to taste. Stir in cheese if using right away. If not, store pesto in the refrigerator for a week, or the freezer for a month.

Kale chimichurri sauce

Makes 2 cups

1 cup finely chopped kale

¼ cup fresh finely chopped herbs of your choice (parsley, oregano, basil, thyme, rosemary)

5 garlic cloves, minced

1½ teaspoons kosher salt

1 teaspoon red chili flakes (chopped fresh chiles work well too)

½ teaspoon black pepper

1 teaspoon lemon zest

3 tablespoons white wine or sherry vinegar

Pinch of sugar

½ cup olive oil

Chimichurri is an herby Argentinian condiment traditionally served with parrillada, a mix of grilled meats. But it's also great with grilled vegetables and as a spread on bread. You can pulse all of the ingredients in a food processor if you are short on time, but chopping each ingredient separately and letting them meld over a period of hours improves both taste and texture. I add kale and reduce the amount of oil typically called for to boost the nutrients and cut the fat.

Mix all ingredients and let them sit at room temperature for least 2 hours before serving. Store in the refrigerator for up to a week.

Carrot top salsa verde

Makes 1 cup

⅓ cup olive oil

⅓ cup finely chopped leafy carrot tops

3 tablespoons finely chopped fresh oregano

2 tablespoons minced shallot or scallions

1 tablespoon Dijon mustard

1 tablespoon minced white anchovy

Kosher salt

1 to 2 teaspoons lemon juice

This recipe came from the chef at a now-defunct restaurant called The Velveteen Habit in South Berwick. I only mention the name of the place for the play on words considering the main ingredient in this salsa. Sweet, leafy carrot greens are mixed with an array of pungent ingredients to make a tangy sauce for summertime grilled meats and fish. It also adds a depth of flavor stirred into quick soups.

Combine oil, carrot tops, oregano, shallot or scallions, mustard and anchovy. Allow mixture to sit for 30 minutes. Add salt and lemon juice to taste. Store in refrigerator for up to 3 days.

Spicy peanut broccoli noodle salad, page 197

Extreme green

Extreme green measures

The bulk of this book has been about everyday steps to green the food a cook eats and serves. It's about about turning those small steps into habits—ordinary ways of doing things in the kitchen. What follows are the extraordinary efforts and tactics embraced by those even more entrenched in the sustainable food movement than I.

Christine

Make garbage salts, sugars, and seeds—trust me

To this day, my husband resents the year I gave away his single-malt Oban Scotch whisky in the form of homemade holiday mustard because I grabbed the wrong decanter. I used his whisky (instead of sherry, as I'd intended) to soak the mustard seeds before whizzing them up in the food processor.

If my social media feed is any indication of what's trendy, flavored salts are way more fashionable now than whisky-laced mustard. *Good Housekeeping*, *Saveur Magazine* and Boston-based *Food Gift Love* author Maggie Battista all tell me how easy it is to make flavored salts that help elevate the taste of everything from simple salads to sassy desserts.

Infusing a salt—or sugar for that matter—with any flavor simply means that you take a dry, flavorful herb, spice, peel, or seed; do something (toast, grind, zest) to release its flavor; mix it with salt (or sugar) and put it in a pretty jar with a label, a bow and a few suggestions for its use.

Since I've got easy access to Maine sea salt, I gave it a go, but with an unusual green spin. My flavorings were vegetable trash (every bit as trendy as flavored salts these days, incidentally). Think of it as Martha Stewart meets Dan Barber, the New York City chef who creates high-end meals like veggie burgers made with pulp left over from juice bars and meatloaf made from an old dairy cow and potatoes deemed unfit for grocery sales.

I was peeling local carrots, beets, celery root and ginger to make a roasted vegetable dish and mulling over what flavors I'd like in a finishing salt to top it off. Since I was roasting them to concentrate their flavor, it hit me: I wanted more carrot, beet, celery root, and ginger flavor! The answer to my own query lay in the washed peelings sitting on the cutting board.

So as the vegetables roasted on a sheet pan on the oven's top shelf, I toasted the peels in separate little piles on a second sheet pan on the bottom one and then combined them with salts. Then I played mix and match until I arrived at flavors that pleased me: carrot ginger and double celery (celeriac peel plus celery seed) salt.

In her book, Battista volunteers great advice on which type of salt works best for which flavors. She says to consider whether you're making a salt to cook with, bake with, or finish a dish with. If you envision the salt being sprinkled on sizzling steak or a rich chocolate truffle, go with a flaky sea salt. If it's intended to season a roasting chicken or top off glazed carrots, a coarse salt is best. If you've got baking in mind, use a fine sea salt.

I think Martha and Dan make a fine team, don't you?

Great trashy marriages

Other garbage salt (or sugar) combinations that work are red beet and coriander; green leek and lemon; Earl Gray and orange; apple and cinnamon; and vanilla bean and black pepper.

Espresso
Beet
Salt
Carrot
ginger
Salt

Roasted and spiced zucchini seeds

My newspaper food editor Peggy Grodinsky developed this recipe—adapted from Martha Stewart's directions for roasted pumpkin seeds—when she found herself alone in the kitchen with a very, very large zucchini, which you'll need for this recipe. The seeds of small zucchini are soft and juicy and will not work here.

Seeds from a giant zucchini

¼ teaspoon ground ginger

¼ teaspoon ground cinnamon

¼ teaspoon ground cumin

Dash cayenne

Sea salt to taste

1 tablespoon sugar, or more to taste

Extra-virgin olive oil

To remove the seeds from your giant zucchini, scrape out the fleshy, seed-riddled center portion of the vegetable. Separate the large, woody seeds from the flesh. Soak in a bowl of water for a few minutes to remove more of the flesh and strings. Bring salted water to a boil, add seeds, and simmer for 10 minutes before draining.

Preheat oven to 250°. Spread drained (but still wet) seeds on a baking sheet. Bake them for 15 minutes.

Meanwhile, combine spices, salt, and sugar. Remove seeds from the oven when they are somewhat dry. Turn oven up to 325°. Drizzle, but don't douse, seeds with olive oil to coat. Sprinkle seeds with spice mixture (you may not need all of it), and mix thoroughly. Bake until seeds are nice and toasty (15 minutes), stirring occasionally. Watch carefully as they can burn easily. Remove from the oven and cool; they will get crispier as they cool.

If you can manage not to snack on them all immediately, store in an airtight container.

Honey, vanilla, and black pepper cantaloupe seeds

Yes, you can eat cantaloupe (and honeydew and galia) seeds. Dried melon seeds are widely used in Middle Eastern and Asian Indian cooking (you can buy big bags full of dried melon seeds in Asian markets) as a soup thickener, a crunchy garnish (especially if they are flavored), and an ingredient in flavored water. Since melons in those hot climates are widely eaten for their flavor and water content, not letting the seeds go to waste is a wise green eating maneuver.

Makes 2 cups

Seeds from two melons (2 cups)

Kosher salt

1 tablespoon butter, melted

1 tablespoon honey

Seeds from half of a vanilla bean

¼ teaspoon finely ground black pepper

½ teaspoon sea salt

Preheat oven to 250°. Place a rack in the middle of oven. Line a baking sheet with parchment paper.

Rinse the seeds and remove any strings. Bring salted water to a boil, add seeds, and simmer for 10 minutes before draining. Pat dry.

Spread drained (but still wet) seeds on a baking sheet. Bake for 15 minutes.

Combine butter, honey, and vanilla bean seeds in a bowl. Add dried seeds and stir to coat them all.

Spread the seeds out on the prepared baking sheet. It's perfectly fine if some touch each other as clumping is okay. Sprinkle with black pepper and salt.

Increase oven temperature to 300°. Roast until seeds are crisp and just start to brown a bit around the edges (15 to 20 minutes). Cool completely. Store in an airtight container.

Garbage finishing salt

Makes 1 cup

1 cup loosely packed root vegetable peels (beets, carrots, celery root, ginger, parsnips)

1 cup salt (Maine sea salt, kosher salt, or flaky Celtic salt)

1 teaspoon complimentary flavoring (cardamom, coriander, celery seed, chili, cinnamon, citrus zest, coffee, tea)

Preheat oven to 300°. Spread root peels on a baking sheet lined with parchment. Bake them until they are dry (30 to 60 minutes depending how thick they are). Cool completely. Use a coffee grinder to pulverize the dried peels. Mix 1 heaping tablespoon with salt and optional, complimentary flavoring. Let sit one day before using. Store in an air-tight container in a dry place.

Raw vanilla ginger finishing sugar

Makes 4 cups

4 cups raw sugar

1 whole vanilla bean, halved and scraped of its seeds

8 (2-inch) pieces of ginger peel

This concoction made from baking ingredient castoffs can elevate everything from a basic cup of tea to a dressed up gingerbread. Sprinkle it liberally around your life. Note: the combination must sit together for at least two weeks before the flavors truly meld and will get stronger the longer the vanilla and ginger are in the jar.

Combine the ingredients in a clean quart mason jar. Cover it with cheese cloth secured with a rubber band. Let sit in a cool, dry spot for at least two weeks. Shake it when you think of it to separate any of the clumps that may have formed. After two weeks, remove flavorings, put a cover on the jar, and keep it with your other sugars.

Christine

Shopping for a waste-free life

I burn fewer calories trekking to collect groceries than I used to because I now remember to grab reusable bags on my way out the kitchen door and don't have to retrace my steps to get them later. This slightly green alteration to my grocery store practice has taken five years to commit to muscle memory.

With my journey toward greener groceries flowing at this glacial pace, I read with amazement about a store in Berlin, Germany, called Original Unverpackt, which "dispenses with disposable packaging." Everything—whether wet or dry—is sold in bulk. If you don't bring your own reusable cloth bags, stainless steel containers and glass jars, they'll sell you one, but your food isn't leaving in a plastic wrapper. Berliners, apparently, are taking this unwrapping in stride. But shopping in that fashion would need to happen in baby steps for me.

I bought a book called *Zero Waste Home*, a memoir/how-to crossover written by Bea Johnson that details how her family has managed to limit its trash in their California home to a quart jar annually. Yes, that's for the entire year, folks. (The average American produces over 4 pounds of trash a day.)

Johnson's simplest shopping strategies include hitting the store only once a week, and taking a list, which she compiles on the back of the previous week's grocery receipt. These steps help a shopper buy only what she needs and use up all she has before getting more. These steps I can manage.

Johnson keeps a few large baskets in her trunk. One is filled with mesh produce bags that give cashiers a clear line of sight to the item stickers, and the other is filled with variously sized cotton drawstring bags to transport items available from bulk bins (flour, sugar, grains, beans, cereal, cookies, nuts).

She uses a permanent marker to label each bag with its "tare" weight (the weight of the empty bag, which gets subtracted from the weight of a filled bag so that a buyer isn't overcharged) and uses a washable marker to label its contents directly on the bag at the store. At home, she pours the goods into see-through, airtight containers, launders the cloth bags, and returns them to the baskets in the trunk.

Expanding my bulk bin use beyond filberts and farro (both are hard to find packaged) will take effort.

Johnson uses a pillowcase to buy bread. Bypassing bread's plastic or paper sleeves may require handing the case over to the baker at the beginning of the trip and collecting your order when you're finished shopping. Easy access to fresh bread on the ride home could be enough inspiration for me to make this step work.

Johnson keeps a rigid tote in her kitchen to store glass bottles needed to carry wet items (milk, yogurt, honey, peanut butter, olive oil, pickles, etc.). She also uses jars to transport items from the meat, fish, and deli counters (the attendant places a price sticker on the jar) instead of picking the same cuts that are pre-wrapped in polystyrene and plastic.

She readily admits you'll need, at first, to explain to butchers and fishmongers why glass is a preferable option for your protein purchases and possibly ensure that your containers are clean, but eventually they will get used to being asked to stuff ground beef into a mason jar, especially if more people like me and you ask them to provide it that way.

Salted dark chocolate and peanut butter popcorn

Most of these ingredients can be bought in bulk, using your own containers. It's a great road trip food too in that it will keep you from buying packaged snacks.

Makes 6 cups

2 tablespoons neutral oil or reserved bacon fat if you've got it

¼ cup popcorn kernels

¼ cup honey

¼ raw sugar

¼ cup unsweetened peanut butter

1 teaspoon fine sea salt

½ teaspoon vanilla

4 ounces good-quality dark chocolate, melted

Heat the oil in a medium pot over medium-high heat. Pour in the corn kernels, cover the pot and shake. As the popcorn pops, shake pan occasionally and remove from the heat once the popping slows to 2 to 3 seconds between pops. Pour popcorn into a large bowl.

Line two baking sheets with parchment paper.

Pour honey and sugar into a small saucepan. Place it over medium heat, bring it to a boil, stirring all the while. Boil it for two minutes. Take the caramel off the heat, stir in peanut butter, salt, vanilla, and chocolate. Pour the mixture over the popcorn and stir to completely coat the popcorn. Spread the popcorn on prepared baking sheets. Let sit at room temperature until caramel and chocolate has hardened (1 hour). Pack in a metal cookie tin with a tight seal.

Christine

Experienced chefs know whey better

Everyone knows Little Miss Muffet took hers with curds, but outside of Mother Goose rhymes, most eaters who knowingly consume whey today—the liquid byproduct of the cheesemaking process—take it in the form of protein bars and smoothies.

If you make your own cheese, you'll find that for every gallon of milk you use you get one quart of cheese curds (the first step to cheese) plus three quarts of whey. The cheese you know what to do with, but is there a use for all that whey? In a word, yes. Many uses.

Chef Ilma Jeil Lopez, who owns Piccolo in Portland with her husband, chef Damien Sansonetti, is keen on putting every drop of the silky, pleasingly sour whey left from making whole-milk ricotta cheese to use in the restaurant's handmade pasta dishes. "No waste in this kitchen," Lopez says.

Lopez and Sansonetti pan-steam potatoes and turnips in whey until they are tender (Whey-Braised Potatoes and Turnips, 193) and then fry them. The whey—which tastes like plain yogurt—adds flavor, while the protein absorbed by the vegetables during steaming turns them especially crispy when fried.

At Vinland, also in Portland, chef David Levi sometimes serves whey-poached parsnips. Also, in keeping with his local foods-only mantra, Levi uses whey to replace (non-local) citrus. This adds an acidic brightness to spicy, garlicky mussels and other dishes.

You can also simply drink it: straight; mixed with lemon juice and a sweetener to make probiotic lemonade or in a boozy cocktail like the Pine Gimlet at Vinland, where it shares the glass with gin and pine syrup.

In baking, whey can replace water in most bread recipes and buttermilk in most cake recipes. Barrington, New Hampshire, homesteader Steve Diamond uses whey to make pancakes. The considerable reaction between the acids in the whey and the baking powder in the batter provides enough leavening power that he can use straight whole wheat flour and still get light and fluffy pancakes.

If you're not making your own cheese, ask a local cheese maker to set aside whey for you, Maine Cheese Guild President Eric Rector suggests. "It is not in short supply," he said, "but by necessity, all cheese makers have developed ways to handle the whey we inevitably produce."

Buy an extra quart—it keeps in the refrigerator for up to 6 days, and freezes really well, too.

Whey-braised potatoes and turnips

A batch of Piccolo's house-made ricotta yields 6 quarts of whey. At the restaurant, chef/owners Ilma Jeil Lopez and Damien Sansonetti use that whey to pan-steam all sorts of vegetables. They often use separate pans to preserve the vegetables' color; we've simplified the procedure for the home cook.

Serves 4 to 6 as a side dish

1 pound medium red potatoes

1 pound small turnips

2 cups whey

Neutral oil

Kosher salt and black pepper

2 tablespoons chopped parsley

Cut the potatoes into quarters. Trim the tops and root ends of the turnips and cut into quarters.

Place the potatoes and turnips in a single layer in a large sauté pan. Add whey. Cover the pan and place over medium-high heat. Pan-steam the vegetables until just tender and still fully intact (10 to 12 minutes). Drain off any whey that has not been absorbed. Set the vegetables aside.

Wipe the sauté pan clean. Place it over high heat and apply a thin coat of oil to the pan. When the pan is hot, add the cooked potatoes and turnips, tossing to coat them with oil. Cook the vegetables undisturbed until the undersides are crispy and slightly browned (4 to 6 minutes). Season with salt and pepper. Garnish with parsley and serve warm.

Christine

From a little acorn, use of mighty good flour could grow

Chris Knapp began a recent class on processing red oak nuts with a beautiful story about how the first tree gifted its acorns to the four- and two-legged creatures sharing the forest in which it thrived.

He told the 20 permaculturists present at the event, sponsored by the Maine Permaculture Resilience Hub, that the four-legged creatures have always consumed these nutrient-dense packages with abandon. But modern Mainers' interest in eating acorns has fallen way off the high mark set by the indigenous people of North America, who used the nut flour in soup, mush, biscuits, and bread.

Knapp has processed a ton of acorns (and I mean that literally), for his family's consumption on their homestead in Temple and to demonstrate the process to attendees at the Koviashuvik Local Living School he operates there. He's hooked on acorn flour because it's locally sourced, yields one pound of flour per two pounds of nuts, and can be substituted for 50 percent of the flour in any bread recipe.

The result will be denser because of the high-fat content of acorns and will taste and smell different because of the flour's very nutty taste and woody scent. "But it will become your new favorite bread recipe," he said.

The only commercially available acorn flour comes from Korea, where it is used in making noodles. Knapp carefully explains to pupils who want to enjoy acorn flour that they've got to make it themselves. Be forewarned: it's an involved process.

Harvesting acorns is a great fall activity. Oaks start dropping their nuts in late September and hold off on dropping their leaves until the all acorns have fallen in early November. Good acorns can be both fat and round and skinny and oval, but they should never be wearing their caps, have pinholes (one means the weevil is still in the nut, two means he came and left), or be black.

Acorns must be passively dried for three to six weeks so they don't mold in storage and so the shells crack easily to start the flour-making process. A sunny windowsill works for small amounts; larger quantities can be spread out in pizza boxes on radiators. Dried acorns can be stored for years.

To crack open the shells, Knapp places a wooden disk in the bottom of a five-gallon bucket, covers it with a layer of acorns and crushes them with a heavy wooden mallet—while singing. Since the nut meat sinks and shells float, the two are easily separated in water. Spreading the meats out on a screen with a ¼-inch weave gives shell pickers a bird's eye view of larger pieces that may have stuck around while tiny fragments fall through.

Knapp runs the nut meats through a $50 Corona corn and grain grinder, as finer grain mills will clog due to the high fat content. He sifts the grind through a series of screens with progressively smaller holes and gets chunks that he fries and salts for snacking, grits that he uses for porridge, and flour for baking.

Still, each of these products is inedible at this juncture because of the acorn's inherent bitter tannins. So the chunks, grits, and flour have to be leached for three days, 12 hours, and eight hours respectively.

Knapp lines a colander with Reemay garden cloth, makes a paste of water and the acorn chunks, grits or flour, and spreads the paste an inch thick over the Reemay. He then runs a steady stream of water to keep the acorn mixture submerged for the requisite period of time. From there, the acorn products can be stored wet in the refrigerator for three weeks and used in most recipes, with a little less liquid than the recipe calls for, or they can be dried or frozen and stored for two months.

Knapp admits the long process is a labor of love. But he contends it's one that honors the oak's gift.

Nutty English muffin called a crumpet

If you're like me and have lots of interesting flours in your cupboard, use either buckwheat, acorn, rye, whole wheat or barley flours for half of the bread flour in this recipe. But never skimp on the 45-minute rise time, or the crumpets will be short on nooks and crannies. You can use the ring tops from wide-mouth mason jars if you don't have metal ring molds. To serve, slather crumpets with jam or honey and butter. Use a toaster to warm any you don't eat immediately.

Makes 8 to 10 crumpets

1 package fast-acting yeast (2¼ teaspoons)

1 teaspoon sugar

1½ cups warm milk (not more than 110°)

2 cups bread flour (or substitute up to 1 cup of buckwheat, acorn, rye or whole wheat flours)

1 teaspoon kosher salt

2 to 3 tablespoons melted butter

Whisk yeast and sugar into warm milk. Combine flour(s) and salt in a medium bowl. Make a well in the middle of the dry ingredients. Pour the milk mixture into the well and stir to make a wet dough. Don't overbeat. Cover the bowl with a clean towel and leave in a warm place for 45 minutes. The batter will rise, forming bubbles, and become sticky.

Brush the insides of the ring molds with melted butter. Put a large heavy-bottomed skillet over medium heat and brush the pan with melted butter. Arrange as many rings as will fit into the pan and when the butter is sizzling, spoon ¼ cup of batter into each ring.

Turn the heat down to low and cook for 10 minutes until the crumpet tops are almost cooked and are dotted with burst bubbles. Lift the rings off with tongs (they will be hot) and flip the crumpets with a palette knife. Cook for 2 minutes more. Set aside on a baking sheet. Re-grease the crumpet rings and repeat the process with remaining mixture.

Serve hot or cool completely and store in an airtight container for toasting later.

Christine

Tweak your own recipes to be leaner, meaner, and cleaner

While a Google search for "blueberry muffin recipe" yields 1.62 billion results, not all will yield a perfect muffin. Some will have too much fat and others not enough flavor. Still more will require too many bowls, and others will omit integral steps.

When I test a recipe, I find its holes using a rubric that ensures all ingredients are accounted for, all instructions flow smoothly, and all results are repeatable. I've started including a green dimension in my testing process. I look for ways to reduce waste in every recipe, both in terms of ingredients and time.

Here's how I make recipes mean (frugal), lean (streamlining processes and conserving natural resources), and clean (minimizing processed foods and dishes).

1. Change ingredient measures to keep ratios proportional but eliminate food waste. For example, blueberry muffins requiring a full cup of blueberries for a recipe that yields four cups of batter is overkill.

2. Learn how to substitute. As a budding cook, I used every ingredient in every recipe down to the letter. If the recipe called for two tablespoons of ancient, Italian, hand-ground-cake flour, I went and bought it at great expense with no plans for using the rest of the 1-pound bag. *The Substitution Bible*, by David Joachim gives me options for using the ingredients I have in my cupboard in place of ones I don't.

3. Understand your appliances, their efficiencies and waste issues, and the energy they use. Knowing the energy draw of your appliances will let you determine if it's more efficient to melt butter for 30 seconds in the microwave in the batter bowl or use the stovetop for three times that span and generate the need to wash another pan.

4. Combine steps whenever possible to save time, energy and resources. For example, use one large measuring cup to both portion and combine wet ingredients (pour the largest volume in first, then lesser volumes thereafter) and beat the eggs into the mixture before adding them to the dry ingredients in the larger mixing bowl.

Finally, it's important to spread the word about your sustainability. For an online recipe, provide a comment on how you've greened it up. At potlucks, talk up the measures taken. In cookbooks, leave notes. Future readers will be happy to know how the recipe evolved over time, treasure your hand-written commentary, and be thankful you took steps to help develop a mainstream sustainable food system.

Spicy peanut broccoli noodle salad

This salad cooks in one pot, can be tailored to include what you have on hand, and will sit happily in a cooler until you're ready to eat it. It's perfect for potlucks.

Serves 4 to 6

1/2 cup smooth peanut butter

1/4 cup low-sodium soy sauce

2 tablespoons rice wine vinegar

2 tablespoons lime juice

2 tablespoons toasted sesame oil

2 large cloves garlic, minced

1 tablespoon grated ginger

1 tablespoon Asian chili garlic paste

2 cups broccoli florets, blanched and shocked

1 (12-ounce) package udon noodles, cooked in the broccoli blanching water, drained and rinsed

2 scallions, thinly sliced

1 small red pepper, cored and thinly sliced

1/4 cup chopped cilantro

2 tablespoons toasted sesame seeds

In a large bowl, whisk together the peanut butter, soy sauce, vinegar, lime juice, sesame oil, garlic, ginger, and chili garlic paste. Let sit 15 minutes. Add the noodles, broccoli, scallions, red pepper, and cilantro. Stir to combine well. Serve at room temperature, garnished with sesame seeds.

Index

Page numbers in *italics* indicate photographs; **boldface** page numbers indicate essays.

N

O

P

Q

R

S

T

U

V